THE
HANDCRAFTED
BURGER

THE HANDCRAFTED BURGER

MASTER THE ART OF CRAFTING THE ULTIMATE GOURMET BURGERS

This edition published by Parragon Books Ltd in 2018
LOVE FOOD is an imprint of Parragon Books Ltd

Parragon Books Ltd
Chartist House
15–17 Trim Street
Bath BA1 1HA, UK
www.parragon.co.uk/love-food
www.parragon.com.au/love-food

ISBN 978-1-4748-9723-5

Printed in China

Edited by Hannah Kelly

Production by Fiona Rhys-Griffith

Introduction by Dominic Utton

New recipes, home economy and food styling by Lincoln Jefferson

Cover photography by Mike Cooper

New recipe photography by Mike Cooper and Al Richardson

Additional images on pages 8–12 courtesy of iStock

NOTES FOR THE READER

This book uses both metric and imperial measurements. Follow the same units of measurement throughout; do not mix metric and imperial. All spoon measurements are level: teaspoons are assumed to be 5 ml, and tablespoons are assumed to be 15 ml. Unless otherwise stated, milk is assumed to be full fat, eggs and individual fruits and vegetables are medium, pepper is freshly ground black pepper and salt is table salt. A pinch of salt is calculated as $1/16$ of a teaspoon. Unless otherwise stated, all root vegetables should be peeled prior to using.

The times given are an approximate guide only. Preparation times differ according to the techniques used by different people and the cooking times may also vary from those given.

Please note that any ingredients stated as being optional are not included in the nutritional values provided. The nutritional values given are approximate and provided as a guideline only, they do not account for individual cooks, scales and portion sizes. The nutritional values provided are per serving or per item.

For best results, use a food thermometer when cooking meat. Check the latest government guidelines for current advice.

Vegetarians and vegans should be aware that some of the ready-made ingredients used in the recipes in this book might contain animal products. Always check the packaging before use.

It is recommended that you do not consume more than 15 g of chia seeds per day.

CONTENTS

THE BURGER REVIVAL

Are burgers the perfect food? There's a pretty good argument that says so. They are quick, cheap and easy to cook, as well as able to be adapted, added to and experimented upon to suit just about any taste… and, of course, and most importantly, they're utterly delicious.

There's an awful lot more to the humble patty and bun than many might think. The recent resurgence in the popularity of the burger is testament to that – from a wealth of dedicated restaurants serving weird and wonderful varieties to its presence on even the most high-class menus, burger lovers have never had it so good.

But you don't need to eat out to enjoy the pleasures of a gourmet burger – and you don't even need to be especially good at cooking to create them. That's where this book comes in. Over the next pages, you're going to find 100 simple recipes for creating your own delicious burgers, sides and sauces at home, as well as an astonishing number of flavour combinations to ensure your creations are every bit as spectacular as anything made in a professional kitchen.

From straight-up Classic Beef Burgers and Pork Belly Sliders, to Bacon-wrapped Chicken Burgers and Turkey Gorgonzola Burgers, creativity is given free rein – and with flavourings including everything from peanut butter or teriyaki sauce to avocado and jackfruit, there really is no limit to what can be done.

Burgers are by no means limited to meat eaters, either – and inside this book you'll find mouth-watering variations on the form, using ingredients as diverse as quinoa, sweet potato, halloumi and beetroot. Who wouldn't be tempted – vegetarian, vegan or otherwise – by a Kale & Black Bean Sloppy Joe Burger, served in a home-made bun with garlic chips and guacamole?

Sides are not forgotten – and move way beyond fries: with easy recipes for salads, coleslaws, onion rings, plus a range of chips that go above and beyond the usual (Smoky Paprika Sweet Potato Fries, anyone?) the whole meal is catered for. There are even simple steps to creating your own ketchups, mustards, salsas, hummus and mayonnaise.

And the best thing? Delicious they may be – but these burgers are not the 'guilty pleasure' you might assume them to be: each recipe also includes a nutritional analysis, so you can see exactly what you're eating. Believe it or not, many are an awful lot healthier than you would think.

Making burgers is not only easy – it's fun. Whether you're selecting the right cuts of meat at the butchers, learning to fashion the perfect patty, experimenting with different cooking methods, getting creative with your sauces, toppings and other ingredients, or whipping up a selection of perfect sides, there's everything you need here to ensure no barbecue, dinner party or family get-together will ever be the same again.

So roll up your sleeves, strap on the apron, turn up the heat and get your taste buds in gear… the following recipes are going to change the way you look at the humble burger forever.

GETTING STARTED

True to its humble origins, the beef burger is a low-tech food requiring not much more than a sharp knife for slicing tomatoes and a frying pan, grill or barbecue. Here is the only equipment you'll really need:

- Mixing bowls
- Spatula for flipping burgers
- Knives for slicing tomatoes (serrated work well), lettuce and other accompaniments
- Whisk for making sauces such as mayonnaise

- Frying pan or griddle pan. Look for heavy-based pans, which have better heat transfer, to create a better sear on your burgers
- Grill pan and rack
- Gas, electric or charcoal barbecue
- Meat mincer or food processor (optional) to make the freshly minced burgers

HOW TO MAKE THE PERFECT BURGER PATTY

Burgers are incredibly easy to prepare, and the only really important step, beyond not overcooking them, is forming the patty. The main thing to avoid is overworking the meat, which can result in tough, rather than tender and juicy, burgers.

Fresh beef mince is the easiest to work with, because it's both dry enough and sticky enough to bind well. Turkey, chicken and pork mince can be much wetter than beef and therefore harder to shape, but adding some breadcrumbs can help alleviate that problem. Also, wetting your hands while forming the patties helps. The same applies to vegetarian burgers, which can be wet and difficult to shape.

To form patties, place the meat in a bowl, add all of the seasonings at once, then mix – preferably with your hands – just until the seasonings are fully integrated.

Divide the meat into portions, then gently form each portion into even-sized patties. If possible, make the patties slightly wider than the buns, because they will shrink during cooking. For the same reason, it also helps to make the edges of the patty thicker than the centre, or to add a dimple to the centre of the patty, so that when the meat contracts, the patty will end up evenly thick when it's cooked.

HOW TO COOK
THE PERFECT BURGER

Quick cooking methods with high, dry heat are the best way to get burgers nicely browned on the outside and juicy inside. Each recipe in this book specifies how to cook the burgers for best results but you can adapt the recipes to use any of the methods listed below.

FRIED AND GRIDDLED

This is the classic diner method of cooking burgers, which involves a hot frying pan and some cooking fat. The burgers cook over a medium–high heat until they develop a golden-brown crust.

STEAMED

Steaming takes frying one step further to keep the meat extra-moist. While frying, just cover the burgers with a lid to finish cooking.

BARBECUED

Charcoal barbecues provide a smoky flavour, but gas ones are easier to use. To check the heat level of your barbecue after preheating, hold your hand about 2.5 cm/1 inch above the cooking grate. The time it takes to get uncomfortably hot determines how hot the grill is:

HIGH: about 3 seconds
MEDIUM–HIGH: about 5 seconds
MEDIUM: about 7 seconds

SMOKED

A foil pouch of wood chips creates smoke that infuses its flavour into burgers cooking in a covered barbecue. Different kinds of wood create a variety of flavours, so experiment. Smoking on a barbecue requires a barbecue with a lid or hood.

GRILLED

Grilling is an easy, low-mess method that works especially well for fish, poultry or vegetarian burgers, which tend to stick to the grill. It is also a great alternative for any recipe that calls for grilling when the weather doesn't say 'outdoor cooking'.

HINTS & TIPS

Choose meat with the right amount of fat. Because burgers cook over a relatively high heat, using lean meat can result in dry, tasteless burgers. The preferred fat amount for beef is 18–22 per cent, and turkey or chicken mince from leg meat is the best choice for poultry burgers when it comes to flavour and texture.

You can mince almost any kind of fresh meat yourself. Beyond beef, you can use the same method with chicken, lamb, pork or turkey. Just cut the meat into 2.5-cm/1-inch cubes and chill first to avoid ending up with puréed meat (particularly important with poultry).

If you prefer your burgers well done, add grated cheese or finely chopped vegetables to the meat to keep it moist. Some people even add chipped ice to their mince, around 2 crushed ice cubes per 450 g/1 lb of meat (these would need to be cooked immediately, for obvious reasons).

Always preheat before cooking. Whether using a frying pan, grill or barbecue, make sure the cooking surface or grill is very hot before you add the burgers. This will prevent sticking and result in the best browning.

Be gentle with the meat. If your burgers come out a bit tough, it means that you probably handled the meat too much when forming the patties.

Choose your buns wisely. Most burger aficionados prefer softer buns or bread that doesn't fight with the meat or vegetable patty. If you like to warm the buns, don't allow them to get too dry and toasty. Have a go at making your own buns on pages 200 and 202.

Don't mess with the burgers. Some cooks like to flip their burgers several times and can't help but press down on them with a spatula. This will only toughen them up.

A few recipes call for an item on the barbecue to be covered. In these instances it is best to use a barbecue that has a fitted lid or hood. Ultimately, this feature enables an intense smoky flavour to penetrate the food and also ensures more even cooking.

If your burger isn't binding – this can be a problem especially with poultry, fish or vegetarian burgers – try adding breadcrumbs to the mixture. Chill the formed burgers for 15 minutes to help them stay together.

The cooking times given for each recipe are for guidance only. Cook your burgers to your liking, but make sure pork and chicken are cooked properly. Cut into the middle to check that the meat is no longer pink. Any juices that run out should be clear and piping hot with visible steam rising.

CHAPTER ONE

MEAT

PEANUT BUTTER BURGER WITH BACON & TOMATO CHILLI JAM

A TWIST ON A CLASSIC AMERICAN SANDWICH, THIS UNIQUE BURGER IS THE PERFECT COMBINATION OF SWEET AND SAVOURY.

 PREP TIME: 10 MINUTES | COOK TIME: 30 MINUTES | SERVES: 4

800g /1 lb 12 oz fresh beef mince

8 streaky bacon rashers

4 brioche burger buns, split

8 large gherkins, sliced

salt and pepper (optional)

TOMATO CHILLI JAM

2 tbsp olive oil

½ red onion, diced

1 garlic clove, crushed

½ tsp chilli flakes

2 tbsp soft light brown sugar

400g/14 oz canned chopped tomatoes

salt and pepper (optional)

PEANUT BUTTER SAUCE

2 tbsp mayonnaise

4 tbsp smooth peanut butter

1. Place the beef mince and salt and pepper, if using, into a large bowl. Using a wooden spoon, mix together, then shape into four equal-sized patties. Press your thumb in the middle of each patty to help keep an even size when cooking. Set aside.

2. To make the jam, heat the oil in a medium-sized pan over a medium heat. Add the onions, garlic and chilli and cook for 5–8 minutes, until slightly golden, stirring frequently. Then add the sugar, tomatoes, salt and pepper, if using. Cook until the jam has reduced by half, this should take around 5 minutes. Remove from the heat and leave to cool.

3. While the jam is cooking, vigorously whisk together the mayonnaise and peanut butter in a bowl to make the sauce, then leave to one side.

4. Heat a large non-stick frying pan over a medium heat, add the bacon rashers and slowly cook until crispy, turning every now and then. Once the bacon is cooked, remove and set aside.

5. Turn up the heat, then add the patties to the large frying pan and cook for 3 minutes on each side, until cooked to your liking.

6. Toast the brioche buns, then spread each side with the peanut butter sauce. Set a burger on top of each base, then top with the jam, gherkins and crispy bacon. Serve immediately.

PER SERVING: 954 KCAL | FAT: 54.6 G | SAT FAT: 18.9 G | CARBS: 56.3 G | SUGARS: 19.5 G | FIBRE: 3.7 G | PROTEIN: 57.1 G | SALT: 2.4 G

SPICY BEEF BURGERS WITH GUACAMOLE

A HINT OF CHILLI ADDS JUST A LITTLE HEAT TO THESE MINCED RUMP STEAK BURGERS BUT YOU CAN ADD MORE SPICE TO SUIT YOUR TASTE.

 PREP TIME: 30 MINUTES, PLUS CHILLING | COOK TIME: 10 MINUTES | SERVES: 4

500 g/1 lb 2 oz rump steak, visible fat removed, diced

½ tsp chilli powder

1 tsp cumin seeds, roughly crushed

½ tbsp fresh thyme leaves

1 tbsp olive oil

4 seeded spelt rolls, split

1 Romaine lettuce heart, shredded

handful of rocket leaves (optional)

2 large tomatoes, sliced

salt and pepper (optional)

GUACAMOLE

1 large avocado, stoned and peeled

juice of 1 lime

2 spring onions, finely chopped

salt and pepper (optional)

1. With the motor running on a food processor, drop in a few pieces of steak at a time, until it has all been roughly chopped. Alternatively, press the pieces through a mincer on the coarse setting.

2. Put the chilli powder, cumin seeds, thyme and a little salt and pepper, if using, in a bowl and mix well. Rub this into the steak, then shape the mixture into four patties. Cover and chill in the refrigerator for 15 minutes.

3. To make the guacamole, put the avocado in a shallow bowl and mash with a fork. Add the lime juice and spring onions, season with a little salt and pepper, if using, and mix well.

4. Preheat the grill to medium–high. Brush the burgers with the oil, then cook, turning halfway through, for 8–10 minutes, or a little less for those who like their burgers pink in the middle. Leave to stand for a few minutes.

5. Meanwhile, toast the rolls, then top the bases with lettuce, rocket, if using, and tomatoes, the hot burgers, and a spoonful of guacamole and the roll lids. Serve immediately.

PER SERVING: 550 KCAL | FAT: 28.7 G | SAT FAT: 6.7 G | CARBS: 36.6 G | SUGARS: 5.6 G | FIBRE: 9.7 G | PROTEIN: 34.7 G | SALT: 0.8 G

CHEESE & BACON BURGERS

THIS AMERICAN DINER CLASSIC FEATURES THE HARD-TO-BEAT COMBINATION OF BEEF, BACON AND CHEESE.

PREP TIME: 15 MINUTES | COOK TIME: 20 MINUTES | SERVES: 4

6 bacon rashers

450 g/1 lb fresh lean beef mince

4 Cheddar cheese slices

4 burger buns, split

2 tbsp mayonnaise

4 Little Gem lettuce leaves

2 large tomatoes, sliced

salt and pepper (optional)

1. Preheat the barbecue to medium–high. Put the bacon in a frying pan over a medium heat and cook for about 8 minutes, or until crisp. Drain on kitchen paper and break the rashers in half.

2. Place the beef in a bowl and season to taste with salt and pepper, if using. Divide into four equal-sized portions and shape each portion into a patty.

3. Place the patties on the rack and cook, covered, for 4 minutes. Turn, top each burger with a slice of cheese, re-cover and cook for a further 4 minutes, or until the burgers are cooked to your liking and the cheese is melted.

4. Spread both halves of the buns with mayonnaise, then place each burger on a bun base. Top with the bacon pieces, lettuce and tomato slices and finish with the top halves of the buns. Serve immediately.

PER SERVING: 553 KCAL | FAT: 27.4 G | SAT FAT: 11.2 G | CARBS: 30.1 G | SUGARS: 4.3 G | FIBRE: 3.6 G | PROTEIN: 43.5 G | SALT: 2.6 G

DOUBLE-DECKER BURGERS

A DOUBLE-DECKER STACKS TWO BEEF PATTIES FOR A HUGE MOUTHFUL OF A BURGER.

 PREP TIME: 20 MINUTES |  COOK TIME: 10 MINUTES | SERVES: 4

900 g/2 lb fresh beef mince

1 tsp salt

½ tsp pepper

2 tbsp olive oil, for brushing

8 Cheddar cheese slices

4 burger buns, split

4 Little Gem lettuce leaves

2 large tomatoes, sliced

1 red onion, sliced

8 gherkins, halved lengthways

1. Place the beef in a medium-sized bowl with the salt and pepper and gently mix to combine. Divide into eight equal-sized portions and shape each portion into a patty no thicker than 1 cm/½ inch – the thinner the better for these burgers.

2. Place a large griddle pan over a medium–high heat. Lightly brush the burgers with oil and cook for about 4 minutes, without moving, until the burgers are brown and release easily from the pan. Turn and cook on the other side for 2 minutes, then put a slice of cheese on top of each burger and cook for a further 2 minutes, or until cooked to your liking.

3. Place a burger on each bun base, then place a second burger on top. Add the lettuce leaves, tomato slices, onion slices and gherkins and serve immediately.

PER SERVING: 834 KCAL | FAT: 47.5 G | SAT FAT: 20.3 G | CARBS: 34.4 G | SUGARS: 6.9 G | FIBRE: 4.3 G | PROTEIN: 63 G | SALT: 3.6 G

CLASSIC BEEF BURGERS

NO BARBECUE IS COMPLETE WITHOUT THE CLASSIC BEEF BURGER. THESE ARE SEASONED WITH ONION, GARLIC AND MUSTARD, BUT YOU CAN MAKE THEM IN THE PURE TRADITION OF STEAK, SALT AND PEPPER, IF YOU WISH.

 PREP TIME: 15 MINUTES, PLUS CHILLING | COOK TIME: 20 MINUTES | SERVES: 4

450 g/1 lb lean rump steak or
topside, freshly minced

1 onion, grated

3 garlic cloves, crushed

2 tsp wholegrain mustard

1 tsp pepper

2 tbsp sunflower oil, for brushing

4 soft burger buns, split

4 tbsp tomato ketchup (optional)

FRIED ONIONS

2 tbsp olive oil

450 g/1 lb onions, finely sliced

2 tsp light muscovado sugar

1. Preheat the barbecue to medium–high. Place the minced steak, onion, garlic, mustard and pepper in a large bowl and mix together thoroughly, squeezing the meat with your hand. Shape into four equal-sized patties, then cover and leave to chill in the refrigerator for 30 minutes.

2. Meanwhile, make the fried onions. Heat the oil in a heavy-based frying pan, add the onions and sauté over a low heat until soft. Add the sugar and cook for a further 8 minutes, stirring occasionally, or until the onions have caramelized. Drain well on kitchen paper and keep warm.

3. To cook the burgers on the barbecue, check they are very firm and brush generously with oil. Place them on the rack and cook for about 5 minutes on each side, or until cooked to your liking.

4. Cook the burger buns on the grill, cut-side down, until lightly toasted. Place the burgers in the buns and top with the onions and tomato ketchup, if using. Serve immediately.

PER SERVING: 532 KCAL | FAT: 25.7 G | SAT FAT: 5.7 G | CARBS: 43.9 G | SUGARS: 10.8 G | FIBRE: 5.3 G | PROTEIN: 29.7 G | SALT: 0.8 G

CLASSIC CHEESEBURGERS

THERE IS SOMETHING ABOUT THE COMBINATION OF A JUICY BEEF BURGER SIMPLY TOPPED WITH MELTED CHEESE THAT IS IRRESISTIBLY DELICIOUS.

PREP TIME: 10 MINUTES | COOK TIME: 10 MINUTES | SERVES: 4

750 g/1 lb 10 oz fresh beef mince
1 beef stock cube
1 tbsp minced dried onion
2 tbsp cold water
2 tbsp sunflower oil, for brushing
55 g/2 oz Cheddar cheese, grated
4 Little Gem lettuce leaves
4 burger buns, split
2 large tomatoes, sliced

1. Place the beef in a large mixing bowl. Crumble the stock cube over the meat, add the dried onion and water and mix well. Divide the meat into four portions, shape each into a ball, then flatten slightly to make a patty of your preferred thickness.

2. Place a griddle pan over a medium–high heat. Lightly brush the burgers with oil and cook for 5–6 minutes. Turn the burgers, sprinkle the cheese over the cooked side and cook for a further 5–6 minutes, or until cooked to your liking.

3. Place the lettuce leaves on the bottom halves of the buns and top with the burgers. Place a couple of tomato slices on top and add the lids. Serve immediately.

PER SERVING: 608 KCAL | FAT: 30.7 G | SAT FAT: 10.1 G | CARBS: 32 G | SUGARS: 4.9 G | FIBRE: 3.9 G | PROTEIN: 47.4 G | SALT: 1.5 G

THE EVERYTHING BURGER

THIS ALL-AMERICAN BURGER IS FILLED WITH COLOURFUL LAYERS OF BACON, AVOCADO, JALAPEÑOS AND COLESLAW.

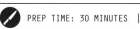 PREP TIME: 30 MINUTES | COOK TIME: 20 MINUTES | SERVES: 4

4 bacon rashers

450 g/1 lb fresh beef mince

1 tbsp vegetable oil, for brushing

4 Monterey Jack cheese slices

4 tbsp Dijon mustard

4 brioche buns, split

pickled jalapeños (optional)

2 large tomatoes, sliced

4 Little Gem lettuce leaves

1 avocado, peeled and thinly sliced

salt and pepper (optional)

COLESLAW

85 g/3 oz red cabbage, shredded

85 g/3 oz hard white cabbage, shredded

55 g/2 oz green cabbage, shredded

2 carrots, about 175 g/6 oz, grated

1 onion, finely sliced

2 red apples, cored and chopped

4 tbsp orange juice

2 celery sticks, finely sliced

4 tbsp low-fat natural yogurt

1 tbsp chopped fresh flat-leaf parsley

1. Put the bacon in a frying pan over a medium heat and cook for about 8 minutes, or until crisp. Drain on kitchen paper and break the rashers in half.

2. Place the beef in a medium-sized bowl with the salt and pepper, if using, and gently mix to combine. Divide into four equal-sized portions and shape each portion into a patty.

3. Place a large frying pan or ridged griddle pan over a medium–high heat. Lightly brush the patties with oil and add them to the pan. Partially cover and cook for about 4 minutes, without moving, until the burgers are brown and release easily from the pan. Turn, place a slice of cheese on top of each burger, partially cover again and cook for a further 3 minutes, or until cooked to your liking.

4. To make the coleslaw, place the cabbage, carrots and onion in a bowl and mix together. Toss the apples in the orange juice and add to the cabbage with any remaining orange juice and the celery. Mix well. Mix the yogurt and parsley in a bowl then pour over the cabbage mixture and stir.

5. Spread the mustard on both halves of the buns and place a few slices of pickled jalapeños on each bun base, if using, and set a burger on top. Then, layer on top of each burger: tomato slices, lettuce leaves, bacon, coleslaw and avocado slices. Serve immediately.

PER SERVING: 823 KCAL | FAT: 41.4 G | SAT FAT: 17.7 G | CARBS: 68.8 G | SUGARS: 21.6 G | FIBRE: 10.4 G | PROTEIN: 45.4 G | SALT: 2.4 G

BARBECUE BURGERS

THIS SIMPLE BEEF BURGER IS FLAVOURED WITH ONION AND GARLIC AND TOPPED WITH A TASTY HOME-MADE BARBECUE SAUCE.

 PREP TIME: 30 MINUTES | COOK TIME: 30 MINUTES | SERVES: 4

450 g/1 lb fresh beef mince

30 g/1 oz onion, finely sliced

1 garlic clove, finely chopped

4 soft burger buns, split

4 Little Gem lettuce leaves

2 large tomatoes, sliced

salt and pepper (optional)

BARBECUE SAUCE

1 tbsp olive oil

1 small onion, finely chopped

2 garlic cloves, crushed

1 fresh red jalapeño chilli, deseeded and finely chopped (optional)

2 tsp tomato purée

1 tsp dry mustard

1 tbsp red wine vinegar

1 tbsp Worcestershire sauce

3 tsp muscovado sugar

300 ml/10 fl oz cold water

1. To make the barbecue sauce, heat the oil in a small, heavy-based saucepan, add the onion, garlic, and chilli, if using, and gently sauté, stirring frequently, for 3 minutes, or until beginning to soften.

2. Blend the tomato purée with the mustard, vinegar and Worcestershire sauce into a paste, then stir into the onion mixture with 2 teaspoons of the sugar. Mix well, then gradually stir in the water.

3. Return to the heat and bring to the boil, stirring frequently. Reduce the heat and gently simmer, stirring occasionally, for 15 minutes. Taste and add the remaining sugar, if liked. Place 125 ml/4 fl oz of the barbecue sauce in a bowl.

4. Preheat the barbecue to medium–high. Place the beef in a medium-sized bowl with the salt and pepper, if using, onion and garlic and gently mix to combine. Divide into four equal portions and shape each portion into a patty.

5. Put the patties on the rack and cook for 4 minutes until brown on one side. Turn, baste with the barbecue sauce and cook for a further 4 minutes, or until cooked to your liking.

6. Spread some of the remaining barbecue sauce on the buns, then place the burgers in the buns. Top with the lettuce leaves and tomato slices and serve immediately.

PER SERVING: 428 KCAL | FAT: 16.4 G | SAT FAT: 5.1 G | CARBS: 38.9 G | SUGARS: 10.4 G | FIBRE: 4.3 G | PROTEIN: 28.6 G | SALT: 0.8 G

SLOPPY JOES

THE SECRET TO A GREAT SLOPPY JOE IS SLOWLY SIMMERING THE BEEF MIXTURE UNTIL IT'S RICH AND TENDER.
YOU SHOULD ALWAYS SERVE SLOPPY JOES WITH A FORK, BUT YOU SHOULD NEVER NEED TO USE IT!

PREP TIME: 10 MINUTES | COOK TIME: 60 MINUTES | SERVES: 4

675 g/1 lb 8 oz fresh lean
beef mince

½ onion, diced

2 garlic cloves, finely chopped

1 red pepper, diced

450 ml/15 fl oz cold water

200 g/6 fl oz tomato ketchup

1½ tbsp soft light brown sugar

1 tsp Dijon mustard

1 tsp Worcestershire sauce

1 tsp salt

½ tsp black pepper

cayenne pepper (optional)

4 burger buns, split

crisps (optional)

1. Put the beef and onions into a large cold frying pan and place over a medium heat. Cook, stirring, breaking up the meat into very small pieces with a wooden spoon, until it begins to brown.

2. Add the garlic and green pepper and cook, stirring, for 2 minutes. Add half the water. Cook until simmering, scraping up any sediment from the base of the pan.

3. Stir in the tomato ketchup, sugar, mustard, Worcestershire sauce, salt, black pepper, cayenne pepper, if using, and the remaining water. Bring to simmering point, reduce the heat to low, and simmer for 30–45 minutes, or until most of the liquid has evaporated and the meat mixture is thick, rich and tender.

4. Spoon the beef mixture onto each bun base. Add the bun lids and serve immediately with crisps, if using.

PER SERVING: 486 KCAL | FAT: 13.2 G | SAT FAT: 5.1 G | CARBS: 48.8 G | SUGARS: 19.2 G | FIBRE: 3.7 G | PROTEIN: 40.9 G | SALT: 3.4 G

CHEESE-STUFFED BURGERS

YOU CAN CHOOSE ANY CHEESE OF YOUR LIKING FOR THIS RECIPE. BE CAREFUL THOUGH – THE MOLTEN FILLING WILL BE VERY HOT WHEN THE BURGERS COME OFF THE BARBECUE.

PREP TIME: 20 MINUTES | COOK TIME: 25 MINUTES | SERVES: 2

325 g/11½ oz fresh beef mince

½ tsp salt

½ tsp pepper

2 Cheddar cheese slices, quartered

1 tbsp vegetable oil, for frying

½ red onion, sliced

2 soft burger buns, split

4 Little Gem lettuce leaves

2 large tomatoes, sliced

1. Preheat the barbecue to medium–high. Place the beef in a small bowl with the salt and pepper and combine. Divide into four equal-sized portions and roll each portion into a ball. Place the balls on a clean work surface and flatten until slightly larger than the buns and about 1 cm/½ inch thick. Arrange the cheese on top of two of the patties, leaving a 1-cm/½-inch border. Add the remaining two patties and firmly press the sides to seal (otherwise the cheese will come out during cooking).

2. Heat the oil in a frying pan over a medium heat. Add the onion slices and fry for about 8 minutes, stirring frequently, until soft and brown. Alternatively, you could barbecue the onion slices for about 2 minutes on each side while you cook the burgers.

3. Place the patties on the rack, rounded side up. Cook for 8 minutes, then carefully turn over and cook on the other side for 5–7 minutes.

4. Place each burger on a bun base, top with the onions, lettuce, tomatoes and the top half of the bun and serve immediately.

PER SERVING: 629 KCAL | FAT: 33.1 G | SAT FAT: 12.5 G | CARBS: 35.6 G | SUGARS: 7 G | FIBRE: 5.2 G | PROTEIN: 44.9 G | SALT: 2.7 G

BLACK & BLUE BURGERS

THESE BURGERS GET THEIR NAME FROM A BLACK PEPPER SPICE RUB AND A BLUE CHEESE DRESSING.

PREP TIME: 30 MINUTES | COOK TIME: 10 MINUTES | SERVES: 4

450 g/1 lb fresh beef mince

4 burger buns, split

4 Little Gem lettuce leaves

2 large tomatoes, sliced

BLUE CHEESE DRESSING

115 g/4 oz blue cheese

50 ml/2 fl oz mayonnaise

50 ml/2 fl oz soured cream

1 shallot, finely chopped

SPICE RUB

1 tsp pepper

1 tsp paprika

1 tsp dried thyme

1 tsp salt

½ tsp cayenne pepper

1. To make the blue cheese dressing, put the cheese, mayonnaise and soured cream into a bowl and mash together until the mixture is as smooth as possible. Add the shallot and stir it into the dressing. Set aside.

2. To make the spice rub, mix the black pepper, paprika, thyme, salt and cayenne pepper together in a small bowl.

3. Divide the beef into four equal-sized portions and shape each portion into a patty. Sprinkle evenly on both sides with the spice rub.

4. Heat a large, non-stick frying pan over a high heat. Add the patties and cook for about 4 minutes until the spice mixture forms a light crust and the edges are brown. Turn and cook on the other side for a further 4 minutes until brown and cooked to your liking.

5. Transfer the burgers to the buns, top with the blue cheese dressing, lettuce leaves and tomato slices and serve immediately.

PER SERVING: 577 KCAL | FAT: 32.9 G | SAT FAT: 12.7 G | CARBS: 33.4 G | SUGARS: 5.2 G | FIBRE: 4.2 G | PROTEIN: 34.7 G | SALT: 3.3 G

STEAKHOUSE BURGERS

THE VERY BEST BURGERS ARE MADE WITH FRESHLY CHOPPED MEAT, AND YOU DON'T NEED A MEAT GRINDER FOR THE TASK.

 PREP TIME: 20 MINUTES, PLUS CHILLING | COOK TIME: 10 MINUTES | SERVES: 4

450 g/1 lb boneless braising steak or a mixture with at least 20 per cent fat

1 tsp salt

½ tsp pepper

4 Gruyère cheese slices

2 tbsp mayonnaise

2 tbsp tomato ketchup

4 burger buns, split

4 Little Gem lettuce leaves

2 large tomatoes, sliced

1. Preheat the barbecue to medium–high. Chop the beef into 2.5-cm/1-inch cubes, then place on a plate, wrap in clingfilm and chill in the refrigerator for about 30 minutes.

2. Place half the beef in a food processor or blender. Pulse (do not run the processor) about 15 times. Season the meat with half the salt and half the pepper, and pulse a further 10–15 times until the meat is finely chopped but not over-processed. Remove from the processor and repeat with the remaining beef. Divide into four equal-sized portions and shape each portion into a patty.

3. Place the patties on the rack and cook until brown and cooked to your liking, 3 minutes on each side for medium-rare and 4 minutes on each side for medium. Place a slice of cheese on each burger during the last 2 minutes of cooking.

4. Meanwhile, put the mayonnaise and ketchup into a small bowl and mix to combine. Spread on the buns, then add the burgers with the lettuce leaves and tomato slices. Serve immediately.

PER SERVING: 639 KCAL | FAT: 40.6 G | SAT FAT: 18.4 G | CARBS: 32.7 G | SUGARS: 6.2 G | FIBRE: 3.7 G | PROTEIN: 34.6 G | SALT: 3 G

SMOKED BURGERS

SMOKED GOUDA CHEESE ADDS EXTRA FLAVOUR TO THESE LIGHTLY SMOKED BEEF BURGERS
AND A SWEET PLUM RELISH MAKES A DELICIOUS ACCOMPANIMENT.

PREP TIME: 15 MINUTES | COOK TIME: 10 MINUTES | SERVES: 4

wood chips, for smoking

450 g/1 lb fresh beef mince

4 smoked Gouda cheese slices

4 brioche buns, split

4 tbsp plum relish

salt and pepper (optional)

1. Soak the wood chips in water for at least 10 minutes.

2. Place the beef in a bowl with the salt and pepper, if using, and gently mix to combine. Divide into four equal-sized portions and shape each portion into a patty.

3. If using a gas barbecue, wrap the drained wood chips in foil, making a pouch but leaving the ends open to allow the smoke to escape. Lift the grate, place the pouch on top of a side burner, and turn the heat to high. Turn the other burners to medium or low, cover and preheat the barbecue to 200°C/400°F.

4. If using a charcoal barbecue, preheat to medium–high. Push the coals to one side and place the wood chips on top.

5. When the wood starts smoking, put the burgers on the rack on the opposite side of the barbecue. Cover and cook for about 4 minutes until brown, then turn and cook on the other side. After 2 minutes, add the cheese and cook for a further 2 minutes, or until the burgers are brown and cooked to your liking.

6. Place the burgers in the buns and top with some of the relish. Serve immediately.

PER SERVING: 571 KCAL | FAT: 26.9 G | SAT FAT: 14.4 G | CARBS: 44.7 G | SUGARS: 10 G | FIBRE: 2.3 G | PROTEIN: 35.2 G | SALT: 1.8 G

PORCINI MUSHROOM BURGERS

DRIED PORCINI MUSHROOMS GROUND TO A POWDER
DELICATELY PERFUME AND SEASON THE BEEF IN THESE BURGERS.

PREP TIME: 10 MINUTES | COOK TIME: 10 MINUTES | SERVES: 4

25 g/1 oz dried porcini mushrooms

2 tbsp olive oil, plus extra for grilling

1 tsp salt

½ tsp pepper

450 g/1 lb fresh beef mince

55 g/2 oz Gruyère cheese, grated

4 brioche buns, split

4 tsp softened butter

caramelized red onion chutney (optional)

1. Grind the mushrooms to a powder in a spice grinder or clean coffee grinder. You should have about 2 tablespoons. Put the powder into a bowl with the oil, salt and pepper and stir until the salt is dissolved. If necessary, add up to 2 teaspoons of water to thin the mixture. Add the beef and gently mix to combine, then divide into four equal-sized portions and form each portion into a patty.

2. Heat a griddle pan over medium–high heat, then coat with the oil. Put the patties in the pan and cover. Cook for about 4 minutes on each side until browned. Turn over, and after 2 minutes, put the cheese on top of the burgers and cook for an additional 2 minutes until the burgers are browned and cooked to your liking.

3. Spread the buns with butter and place the burgers in the buns. Top with the onion chutney, if using, and serve immediately.

PER SERVING: 655 KCAL | FAT: 38 G | SAT FAT: 16.1 G | CARBS: 40.8 G | SUGARS: 5.4 G | FIBRE: 3.2 G | PROTEIN: 34.7 G | SALT: 2.5 G

AUSSIE BURGERS

A CLASSIC AUSTRALIAN COMBINATION OF BEETROOT, GRILLED PINEAPPLE AND A FRIED EGG MAKE THIS MILE-HIGH BURGER EXTRA SATISFYING.

PREP TIME: 20 MINUTES | COOK TIME: 12 MINUTES | SERVES: 4

450 g/1 lb fresh beef mince

3 tbsp vegetable oil, for brushing and frying

4 pineapple slices

4 medium eggs

4 soft burger buns, split

4 tbsp mayonnaise

8 beetroot slices in vinegar

4 Little Gem lettuce leaves

2 large tomatoes, sliced

salt and pepper (optional)

1. Place the beef in a medium-sized bowl with salt and pepper, if using. Mix gently to combine, then divide into four equal-sized portions and shape each portion into a patty.

2. Place a griddle pan over a medium–high heat and add 1 tablespoon of the oil. Lightly brush the patties and pineapple slices with 1 tablespoon of oil and place the patties and pineapple in the pan. Cover and cook the pineapple for 3 minutes on each side until each slice is soft and marked, and cook the burgers for about 4 minutes on each side until brown and cooked to your liking. Remove from the heat and keep warm.

3. Add 1 tablespoon of oil to a frying pan, swirling to coat the pan. Add the eggs and season to taste with salt and pepper, if using. Cover and cook for about 3 minutes until the whites are set and the yolks are beginning to set at the edges.

4. Spread some mayonnaise on each half of the buns. Place a pineapple slice and a lettuce leaf on each bun base, then add a burger, 2 beetroot slices, tomato slices and an egg. Finish with the bun tops and serve immediately.

PER SERVING: 663 KCAL | FAT: 38 G | SAT FAT: 8.8 G | CARBS: 42.4 G | SUGARS: 12.8 G | FIBRE: 4.9 G | PROTEIN: 34.9 G | SALT: 1.3 G

BEEF TERIYAKI BURGERS

TERIYAKI SAUCE IS USED AS A MARINADE TO TENDERIZE THE BEEF AND INFUSE IT WITH SOME ORIENTAL FLAVOURS.

 PREP TIME: 10 MINUTES, PLUS CHILLING | COOK TIME: 10 MINUTES | SERVES: 4

450 g/1 lb fresh steak mince

8 spring onions, chopped

4 garlic cloves, chopped

2.5-cm/1-inch piece fresh ginger, grated

½ tsp wasabi paste

3 tsp teriyaki sauce or teriyaki marinade

2 tbsp peanut oil

115 g/4 oz carrot, grated

115 g/4 oz pak choi, shredded

55 g/2 oz cucumber, shredded

4 burger buns, split

crispy fried seaweed, to garnish (optional)

1. Place the steak mince, spring onions, garlic, ginger, wasabi and teriyaki sauce in a food processor or blender and, using the pulse button, blend together. Shape into four equal-sized patties, then cover and leave to chill in the refrigerator for 30 minutes.

2. Heat a heavy-based frying pan over a medium–high heat and add 1 tablespoon of the oil. When hot, add the patties and cook over a medium heat for 3–5 minutes on each side or until cooked to your liking. Keep warm.

3. Place the carrot, pak choi, cucumber and the remaining oil in a small bowl and mix together.

4. Spoon a little of the vegetables onto the bun bases and top with the burgers and seaweed, if using. Add the bun lids and serve immediately.

PER SERVING: 444 KCAL | FAT: 18.9 G | SAT FAT: 5.3 G | CARBS: 36.7 G | SUGARS: 7 G | FIBRE: 4.7 G | PROTEIN: 29.5 G | SALT: 1.1 G

CHILLI-GARLIC SAUCE BURGERS

A MIXTURE OF BEEF AND PORK MINCE ADDS A DISTINCTIVE FLAVOUR TO THESE BURGERS AND THE CHILLI-GARLIC SAUCE PACKS A REAL PUNCH.

 PREP TIME: 20 MINUTES, PLUS CHILLING | COOK TIME: 20 MINUTES | SERVES: 4

25 g/1 oz fresh coriander
1 garlic clove, finely chopped
225 g/8 oz fresh beef mince
225 g/8 oz fresh pork mince
2 tbsp red chilli sauce
2 tsp fresh ginger, finely grated
2 tsp soy sauce
2 small pak choi
2 tsp vegetable oil
4 burger buns, split

1. Finely chop half of the coriander leaves and place into a large bowl with the garlic, beef, pork, chilli sauce, ginger and soy sauce and mix to combine. Divide the mixture into four equal-sized portions and shape each portion into a 1–2-cm/ ½–¾-inch thick patty. Cover and chill in the refrigerator for 30 minutes.

2. Roughly chop the pak choi, discarding the thick ends. Place a large frying pan over a high heat and add the oil, swirling to cover the base of the pan. Add the pak choi and cook, stirring frequently, until wilted. Set aside.

3. Place the patties in the frying pan and cook for about 4 minutes until brown. Turn and cook for a further 4 minutes until they are cooked through and brown on both sides.

4. Place a patty on the bottom half of each bun. Top with some sautéed pak choi, the whole coriander leaves and the top halves of the buns. Serve immediately.

PER SERVING: 427 KCAL | FAT: 21.3 G | SAT FAT: 7 G | CARBS: 30.1 G | SUGARS: 3.8 G | FIBRE: 3.6 G | PROTEIN: 26.6 G | SALT: 1.3 G

COFFEE BURGERS

COFFEE ADDS A PUNCH OF FLAVOUR TO THESE BEEF BURGERS, AS WELL AS A CAFFEINE HIT!

PREP TIME: 15 MINUTES | COOK TIME: 20 MINUTES | SERVES: 4

1 tbsp instant coffee granules, finely ground

2 tsp soft light brown sugar

1 tsp salt

¼ tsp pepper

500 g/1 lb 2 oz fresh beef mince

1 small onion, grated

1 egg yolk

1 tbsp olive oil, for brushing

4 soft burger buns, split

4 tbsp mayonnaise

1 tsp smooth mustard

100 g/3½ oz peppery salad leaves

2 large tomatoes, sliced

1. Put the coffee, sugar, salt and pepper into a large bowl and mix together. Add the beef, onion and egg yolk and mix together with your hands until thoroughly combined. Divide the mixture into four portions and shape each portion into a patty.

2. Preheat a griddle pan or cast-iron frying pan to medium–high. Lightly brush the burgers with oil and cook for 6–8 minutes on each side, or until cooked through. Alternatively, cook under a hot grill.

3. To serve, lightly toast the burger buns. Mix the mayonnaise and mustard together. Put some salad leaves, tomato slices and a burger on top of four bun halves. Add a dollop of mustard mayonnaise and top with the remaining bun halves. Serve immediately.

PER SERVING: 543 KCAL | FAT: 28.5 G | SAT FAT: 7.6 G | CARBS: 36.2 G | SUGARS: 8.2 G | FIBRE: 4.2 G | PROTEIN: 32 G | SALT: 2.5 G

TURKISH LAMB BURGERS WITH AUBERGINE

THESE LIGHTLY SPICED BURGERS, SERVED BETWEEN THICK, MEATY SLICES OF AUBERGINE WITH A SIDE OF A TRADITIONAL TURKISH SAUCE, WILL HAVE YOU COMING BACK TO THIS RECIPE TIME AND AGAIN.

 PREP TIME: 15 MINUTES | COOK TIME: 20 MINUTES | SERVES: 2

225 g/8 oz fresh lamb mince

2 garlic cloves, crushed

1 tsp ground cumin

1 tsp sumac

1 small egg, beaten

1½ tbsp olive oil

½ large red pepper, deseeded and quartered

1 small onion, thinly sliced into rings

4 large round aubergine slices, each about 1–1½ cm/½–¾ inch thick

2 tsp olive oil, for brushing

salt and pepper (optional)

2 frisée lettuce leaves, to serve

CAÇIK

10-cm/4-inch piece cucumber

3 tbsp thick natural Greek yogurt

2 tsp chopped fresh dill

1 tsp white wine vinegar

¼ tsp salt

1. Add the mince, half the garlic, all the cumin and sumac, the egg and salt and pepper to taste, if using, to a bowl. Combine well and shape into two thick burgers. Set aside.

2. Heat 1 tablespoon of the oil in a non-stick frying pan over a medium–high heat. Add the red pepper and onion rings and cook for 3–4 minutes until soft and slightly charred all over. Transfer to a warmed plate with a slotted spoon. Add the aubergine slices to the pan with the remaining oil and cook for 2–3 minutes on each side until slightly soft and brown. Transfer to the plate with the pepper and onion and season to taste with salt and pepper, if using.

3. To make the caçik, cut the cucumber in half lengthways and deseed. Lightly peel, leaving some green skin, then finely chop. Place on a clean tea towel, wrap and squeeze out as much of the juice as possible. Put the cucumber in a bowl with the yogurt, the remaining garlic and the dill, vinegar and salt.

4. Brush the pan with oil and heat until very hot. Add the lamb burgers and cook, without moving around, for 4–5 minutes on each side, or until cooked through.

5. To assemble each burger, put a slice of aubergine on a serving plate, top with a lettuce leaf, a red pepper slice and a little onion, followed by the lamb burger. Add the remaining red pepper and onion slices, then add a spoonful of the caçik. Top with another aubergine slice. Serve the remaining yogurt sauce on the side.

PER SERVING: 549 KCAL | FAT: 40.9 G | SAT FAT: 15 G | CARBS: 15.4 G | SUGARS: 7.5 G | FIBRE: 4.1 G | PROTEIN: 31.3 G | SALT: 1.1 G

LAMB BURGERS WITH TZATZIKI & FETA

THESE LAMB BURGERS ARE DELICIOUS – THE SWEET TZATZIKI, TANGY PICKLED ONIONS AND SALTY FETA CHEESE ARE THE PERFECT ACCOMPANIMENTS.

 PREP TIME: 15 MINUTES | COOK TIME: 10 MINUTES | SERVES: 4

500 g/1 lb 2 oz fresh lamb mince

1 tsp cumin seeds

1 tbsp vegetable oil, for brushing

4 burger buns, split

100 g/3½ oz feta cheese, crumbled

salt and pepper (optional)

TZATZIKI

4 tbsp Greek-style yogurt

25 g/1 oz fresh mint, chopped

25 g/1 oz fresh dill, chopped

½ cucumber, sliced

salt and pepper (optional)

PICKLED ONIONS

1 red onion, sliced

2 tbsp red wine vinegar

½ tsp salt

1. Preheat the barbecue to medium–high and brush the barbecue rack with a little oil. To make the burgers, mix the lamb, cumin seeds and salt and pepper, if using, together in a medium-sized bowl.

2. Divide the mixture into four equal-sized balls, then shape into patties.

3. To make the tzatziki, mix all of the ingredients together in a small bowl and stir to combine.

4. To make the pickled onions, mix the onion, vinegar and salt together in a separate small bowl.

5. Cook the burgers on the barbecue for 5 minutes on each side, or until cooked through.

6. Divide the burgers between the buns and top with the tzatziki, feta cheese and pickled onions. Serve immediately.

PER SERVING: 623 KCAL | FAT: 36.1 G | SAT FAT: 17.6 G | CARBS: 35.4 G | SUGARS: 6.6 G | FIBRE: 4.1 G | PROTEIN: 37.7 G | SALT: 2.3 G

HERBED LAMB BURGERS

SOMETIMES, THE SIMPLICITY OF FRESH HERBS IS ALL YOU NEED TO MIX WITH LAMB TO CREATE A FLAVOURSOME BURGER.

PREP TIME: 10 MINUTES | COOK TIME: 8 MINUTES | SERVES: 4

450 g/1 lb fresh lean lamb mince

75 g/2¾ oz fresh breadcrumbs

1 onion, finely chopped

3 tbsp chopped fresh herbs, such as mint, rosemary or thyme

1 egg, beaten

½ tbsp apple juice

2 tbsp vegetable oil

4 Little Gem lettuce leaves

4 burger buns, split

2 large tomatoes, sliced

salt and pepper (optional)

1. Place the lamb in a large mixing bowl. Add the breadcrumbs, onion, chopped herbs, egg and apple juice. Season to taste with salt and pepper, if using, and mix together.

2. Divide the mixture into four equal-sized portions, shape each portion into a ball, then flatten slightly to make a burger shape of your preferred thickness.

3. Place a large frying pan over a medium–high heat and add the oil. When hot, add the burgers and cook for 3–4 minutes on each side, until cooked through.

4. Place the lettuce leaves on the bottom halves of the buns and top with the tomato slices. Place the burgers on top and add the lids. Serve immediately.

PER SERVING: 603 KCAL | FAT: 32.6 G | SAT FAT: 12.9 G | CARBS: 42.4 G | SUGARS: 6.7 G | FIBRE: 4.9 G | PROTEIN: 33.2 G | SALT: 1.2 G

MOROCCAN LAMB BURGERS

THESE BURGERS GET THEIR DISTINCTIVE FLAVOUR FROM
AN AROMATIC BLEND OF SPICES AND SPICY HARISSA SAUCE.

 PREP TIME: 20 MINUTES, PLUS STANDING | COOK TIME: 12 MINUTES | SERVES: 4

550 g/1 lb 4 oz fresh lamb mince

1 onion, finely chopped

1 tsp harissa sauce

1 garlic clove, crushed

2 tbsp chopped fresh mint

½ tsp cumin seeds, crushed

½ tsp paprika

2 tbsp olive oil, for brushing

4 pittas, warmed and split

½ red onion, sliced

salt and pepper (optional)

handful of rocket leaves (optional)

YOGURT & CUCUMBER SAUCE

½ large cucumber

1 tsp salt

4 tbsp natural yogurt

6 tbsp chopped fresh mint

1. Preheat the barbecue to medium–high. To make the sauce, peel the cucumber, quarter lengthways and scoop out the seeds. Chop the flesh and put in a sieve set over a bowl. Sprinkle with salt, cover with a plate and weigh down with a can of vegetables. Leave to drain for 30 minutes, then mix with the remaining ingredients.

2. Meanwhile, combine the lamb, onion, harissa sauce, garlic, mint, cumin seeds and paprika. Season to taste with salt and pepper, if using, mixing well with a fork. Divide into four equal-sized portions and flatten into patties about 2.5 cm/1 inch thick. Cover and leave to stand at room temperature for 30 minutes.

3. Lightly brush the burgers with oil. Grease the grill rack. Cook for 5–6 minutes on each side, or until cooked through.

4. Stuff the burgers into the pittas with the red onion slices, rocket leaves, if using, and a spoonful of the sauce. Serve immediately.

PER SERVING: 642 KCAL | FAT: 36.1 G | SAT FAT: 15.4 G | CARBS: 41.2 G | SUGARS: 4.6 G | FIBRE: 3.3 G | PROTEIN: 36.9 G | SALT: 2.7 G

PORK BELLY SLIDERS WITH KIMCHI SLAW

SLIDERS ARE SMALL BURGERS AND ARE GREAT TO SERVE UP AT A DINNER PARTY. THESE JAPANESE-INSPIRED PORK BELLY SLIDERS MIGHT BE SMALL IN SIZE BUT THEY'RE BIG ON FLAVOUR.

PREP TIME: 20 MINUTES | COOK TIME: 2 HOURS 15 MINUTES | MAKES: 14

1 kg/2 lb 4 oz pork belly

3 star anise

1 cinnamon stick

5 dried shiitake mushrooms

5 spring onions

200 g/7 oz sugar

100 ml/3½ fl oz light soy sauce

300 ml/10 fl oz rice wine

100 ml/3½ fl oz rice vinegar

14 slider buns, split

6 tbsp Japanese mayonnaise, for spreading

KIMCHI SLAW

3 tbsp Japanese mayonnaise

½ Chinese cabbage, finely sliced

200 g/7 oz kimchi, sliced

4 spring onions, sliced

20 g/¾ oz pickled ginger, chopped

1. Preheat the oven to 180°C/350°F/Gas Mark 4.

2. Place the pork belly, star anise, cinnamon stick, mushrooms, spring onions, sugar, soy sauce, rice wine and rice vinegar in a baking dish. Cover with greaseproof paper and foil.

3. Roast in the preheated oven for 2 hours, or until the centre of the meat is no longer pink and the juices run clear when the thickest part of the meat is pierced with a skewer. Leave to cool completely in the cooking liquor.

4. To make the slaw, mix all the ingredients together in a medium-sized bowl.

5. Preheat the barbecue to medium–high. Slice the pork into 2 cm/¾ inch thick slices. Place the slices on the barbecue rack and cook for 3–4 minutes on each side, or until starting to caramelize.

6. Cut the pork slices into squares. Spread each bun half with mayonnaise, then fill with the pork squares and top with slaw.

PER SERVING: 415 KCAL | FAT: 34.3 G | SAT FAT: 10.7 G | CARBS: 19.1 G | SUGARS: 5 G | FIBRE: 1.1 G | PROTEIN: 11.8 G | SALT: 0.8 G

BARBECUED CAJUN PORK BURGERS

THE CAJUN SEASONING REALLY LIVENS UP THE FLAVOUR
OF THESE PORK BURGERS, AND GRATED APPLE KEEPS THEM JUICY.

 PREP TIME: 20 MINUTES, PLUS CHILLING | COOK TIME: 35-40 MINUTES | SERVES: 4

1tsp salt

225 g/8 oz sweet potatoes, cut into chunks

450 g/1 lb fresh pork mince

1 apple, peeled, cored and grated

2 tsp Cajun seasoning

2 onions

1 tbsp chopped fresh coriander

2 tbsp sunflower oil

8 lean back bacon rashers

salt and pepper (optional)

1. Bring a saucepan of lightly salted water to the boil, add the sweet potatoes and cook for 15–20 minutes, or until soft when pierced with a fork. Drain well, then mash and reserve.

2. Place the pork in a bowl, add the mashed potato, apple and Cajun seasoning. Grate 1 onion and add to the pork mixture with the coriander, and salt and pepper, if using. Mix together, then shape into four equal-sized patties. Cover and leave to chill in the refrigerator for 1 hour.

3. Slice the remaining onion. Heat 1 tablespoon of the oil in a frying pan. Add the onions and cook over a low heat for 10–12 minutes, stirring until soft. Remove the pan from the heat and reserve. Wrap each patty in 2 bacon rashers.

4. Preheat the barbecue to medium–high. Brush the patties with the remaining oil and cook for 4–5 minutes on each side, or until thoroughly cooked. Serve immediately with the fried onions.

PER SERVING: 547 KCAL | FAT: 36.9 G | SAT FAT: 11.9 G | CARBS: 21.2 G | SUGARS: 7.8 G | FIBRE: 3.3 G | PROTEIN: 32 G | SALT: 2.7 G

SPICY PULLED PORK BURGERS

TENDER, MOIST AND FLAVOURED WITH A BARBECUE-STYLE SAUCE,
THIS SHREDDED PORK IS COOKED FOR 8 HOURS IN A SLOW COOKER.

PREP TIME: 20 MINUTES | COOK TIME: 8 HOURS | SERVES: 6

2 onions, sliced

1.5 kg/3 lb 5 oz boned and rolled
pork shoulder

2 tbsp demerara sugar

2 tbsp Worcestershire sauce

1 tbsp American mustard

2 tbsp tomato ketchup

1 tbsp cider vinegar

4 burger buns, split

salt and pepper (optional)

1. Put the onions in the slow cooker and place the pork on top. Mix together the sugar, Worcestershire sauce, mustard, ketchup and vinegar and spread all over the surface of the pork. Season to taste with salt and pepper, if using. Cover and cook on low for 8 hours.

2. Remove the pork from the slow cooker and use two forks to pull it apart into shreds.

3. Skim any excess fat from the juices and stir a little juice into the shredded pork. Serve in burger buns, with the remaining juices for spooning over.

PER SERVING: 651 KCAL | FAT: 18 G | SAT FAT: 5.4 G | CARBS: 39.2 G | SUGARS: 11.8 G | FIBRE: 2.3 G | PROTEIN: 82.2 G | SALT: 1.5 G

PORK & ORANGE BURGERS

THE PIQUANT FLAVOUR OF ORANGE JUICE AND RIND IS THE MAKING OF THIS BURGER, AND THE ORANGE PEEL IN THE MARMALADE ADDS EXTRA TEXTURE.

 PREP TIME: 45 MINUTES, PLUS CHILLING | COOK TIME: 45 MINUTES | SERVES: 4

450 g/1 lb pork fillet, cut into small pieces

225 g/8 oz parsnips, cut into chunks

1 tbsp finely grated orange rind

2 garlic cloves, crushed

6 spring onions, finely chopped

1 courgette, grated

1 tbsp sunflower oil

4 Little Gem lettuce leaves

4 burger buns, split

salt and pepper (optional)

ORANGE MARINADE

3 tbsp Seville orange marmalade

2 tbsp orange juice

1 tbsp balsamic vinegar

1. To make the marinade, place the marmalade, orange juice and vinegar in a small saucepan and heat, stirring, until the marmalade is runny. Place the pork in a shallow dish and pour the marinade over the pork. Cover and leave for at least 30 minutes. Remove the pork, reserving the marinade. Mince the pork pieces in a large bowl.

2. Meanwhile, cook the parsnips in a saucepan of boiling water for 15–20 minutes, or until tender. Drain, then mash and add to the pork. Stir in the orange rind, garlic, spring onions, courgette and salt and pepper, if using. Mix together, then shape into four equal-sized burgers. Cover and leave to chill in the refrigerator for at least 30 minutes.

3. Preheat the barbecue to medium–high. Lightly brush each burger with the oil and then add them to the barbecue grill, cooking for 4–6 minutes on each side, or until cooked through. Boil the reserved marinade for at least 5 minutes, then pour into a small jug or bowl.

4. Place the lettuce leaves on the bottom halves of the burger buns and top with the burgers. Spoon over a little of the hot marinade, then top with the lids and serve immediately.

PER SERVING: 438 KCAL | FAT: 11.2 G | SAT FAT: 2.7 G | CARBS: 53.7 G | SUGARS: 17.7 G | FIBRE: 7.1 G | PROTEIN: 29.8 G | SALT: 0.8 G

BANH MI-STYLE BURGERS

INSPIRED BY VIETNAMESE BAGUETTE SANDWICHES, THESE FRAGRANT BURGERS ARE PREPARED WITH CHINESE FIVE-SPICE POWDER AND THEN STUFFED INTO BURGER BUNS WITH PICKLED VEGETABLES.

 PREP TIME: 30 MINUTES, PLUS MARINATING | COOK TIME: 10 MINUTES | SERVES: 4

450 g/1 lb fresh pork mince

1 garlic clove, finely chopped

1 tbsp Thai fish sauce

1 tsp Chinese five-spice powder

½ tsp sugar

¼ tsp pepper

50 ml/2 fl oz mayonnaise

4 burger buns, split

½ cucumber, thinly sliced

1 fresh jalapeño chilli, thinly sliced

15 g/½ oz fresh coriander sprigs

2 tbsp soy sauce

PICKLED VEGETABLES

150 g/5½ oz carrots, cut into julienne strips

200 g/7 oz mooli, cut into julienne strips

1 tsp sugar

175 ml/6 fl oz distilled vinegar

175 ml/6 fl oz water

1 tsp salt (optional)

1. To make the pickled vegetables, put the carrots and mooli in a medium-sized bowl and toss with the sugar and salt, if using. Add the vinegar and water and leave to marinate in the refrigerator for at least 30 minutes or overnight.

2. Place the pork, garlic, fish sauce, spice powder, sugar and pepper in a medium-sized bowl and combine. Stir gently, then divide into four equal-sized portions and shape each portion into a patty.

3. Place a ridged griddle pan over a medium–high heat, add the patties and cook for 5 minutes on each side until brown and cooked through.

4. Spread the mayonnaise on the buns and stuff each with a burger, cucumber slices and a few chilli slices. Top with some pickled vegetables and coriander. Drizzle with soy sauce and serve immediately.

PER SERVING: 590 KCAL | FAT: 34.7 G | SAT FAT: 10.5 G | CARBS: 39.8 G | SUGARS: 9.7 G | FIBRE: 5.3 G | PROTEIN: 25.9 G | SALT: 3.3 G

CHAPTER TWO

POULTRY

TURMERIC CHICKEN BURGER WITH TANDOORI MAYO

AN INDIAN-INSPIRED CHICKEN BURGER ACCOMPANIED BY A LIGHT AND MILDLY SPICED SLAW.

 PREP TIME: 10 MINUTES, PLUS MARINADE | COOK TIME: 20 MINUTES | SERVES: 4

2 tbsp vegetable oil

1 tsp ginger, grated

1 tsp garlic, crushed

½ tsp turmeric powder

4 chicken breasts, skin removed

4 burger buns, split

salt and pepper (optional)

TANDOORI MAYONNAISE

6 tbsp mayonnaise

1 tbsp tandoori masala powder

1 tbsp lemon juice

COLESLAW

½ red onion, finely sliced

50 g/1¾ oz white cabbage, finely sliced

50g /1¾ oz red cabbage, finely sliced

1 small carrot, finely sliced

10 g/¼ oz fresh coriander leaves

28 g/10 oz coconut flesh, finely grated

½ tsp cumin seeds

1. Mix together the oil, ginger, garlic, turmeric powder and salt and pepper, if using, in a large bowl to make a marinade. Add the chicken breasts and mix together, then cover with clingfilm and leave in the refrigerator for 2 hours.

2. To make the tandoori mayonnaise, mix together the mayonnaise, tandoori powder and lemon juice in a small bowl.

3. To make the coleslaw, mix together all the ingredients in a medium-sized bowl.

4. Preheat a large griddle pan to medium–high. Remove the chicken from the refrigerator and drain off the excess marinade.

5. Once the griddle pan is hot, add the chicken breasts and cook for 8 minutes on each side, or until thoroughly cooked.

6. Toast the burger buns, then spread with the tandoori mayonnaise.

7. Place a chicken breast on each bun base and top with the coleslaw and bun lid. Serve immediately.

PER SERVING: 544 KCAL | FAT: 28.1 G | SAT FAT: 5.9 G | CARBS: 35.4 G | SUGARS: 5.7 G | FIBRE: 5.5 G | PROTEIN: 34.9 G | SALT: 1.1 G

BUTTERMILK CHICKEN BURGERS WITH SPICY SLAW

CRISPY BUTTERMILK CHICKEN BURGERS AND CRUNCHY, CREAMY, SPICY COLESLAW ARE A MATCH MADE IN HEAVEN.

PREP TIME: 20 MINUTES | COOK TIME: 6 MINUTES | SERVES: 4

4 chicken breast fillets, each about 1 cm/½ inch thick

225 ml/8 fl oz buttermilk

125 g/4½ oz plain flour

1 tbsp smoked paprika

2 tsp garlic powder

½ tsp cayenne pepper

125 ml/4 fl oz vegetable oil

4 tbsp mayonnaise

4 burger buns, split

2 large tomatoes, sliced

4 Little Gem lettuce leaves

salt and pepper (optional)

SPICY SLAW

125 ml/4 fl oz wine vinegar

125 ml/4 fl oz mayonnaise

2 tbsp soured cream

2 tbsp sugar

¾ tsp salt

1 tsp hot sauce

½ tsp pepper

¼ tsp cayenne pepper

½ red onion, thinly sliced

100 g/3½ oz red cabbage, shredded

100 g/3½ oz white cabbage, shredded

2 carrots, grated

1. Place the chicken breasts in a bowl with the buttermilk and toss to coat. Set to one side.

2. To make the spicy slaw, combine the vinegar, mayonnaise, soured cream, sugar, salt, hot sauce, pepper and cayenne pepper. Add the onion, cabbage and carrot to the dressing and toss to coat.

3. Put the flour into a shallow bowl and add the paprika, garlic powder, cayenne pepper and salt and pepper, if using. Stir to mix. Remove the chicken fillets, one at a time, from the buttermilk and dip them in the flour mixture. Return to the buttermilk and dip again in the flour mixture. Heat the oil in a large frying pan over a medium—high heat until very hot. Add the chicken in a single layer and cook for about 3 minutes on each side, until golden brown and cooked through.

4. Spread mayonnaise on the top half of each bun. Place a tomato slice and a lettuce leaf on the base of each bun. Top with a chicken fillet. Serve immediately with the coleslaw on the side.

PER SERVING: 965 KCAL | FAT: 53.4 G | SAT FAT: 9 G | CARBS: 76.5 G | SUGARS: 19.8 G | FIBRE: 8.3 G | PROTEIN: 41.8 G | SALT: 2.9 G

BACON-WRAPPED CHICKEN BURGERS WITH GRILLED PINEAPPLE

THESE BURGERS ARE A REAL MIX OF GORGEOUS FLAVOURS, WITH THE CHICKEN, BACON, PINEAPPLE AND RUSSIAN DRESSING ALL PACKING A PUNCH.

 PREP TIME: 20 MINUTES | COOK TIME: 25 MINUTES | SERVES: 4

8 smoked pancetta rashers

4 skinless, boneless chicken breasts

1 tbsp vegetable oil, for brushing

1 Little Gem lettuce, shredded

4 brioche burger buns, split

GRILLED PINEAPPLE

½ pineapple, peeled

1 tbsp demerara sugar

1 tsp pepper

RUSSIAN DRESSING

3 tbsp mayonnaise

1 tbsp tomato ketchup

1 tbsp horseradish

2 tsp hot pepper sauce

1 tbsp Worcestershire sauce

1 shallot, grated

1. Lay two pancetta rashers next to each other on a chopping board. Place a chicken breast on top of the rashers and wrap the rashers all the way around the breast. Repeat with the remaining breasts.

2. To make the grilled pineapple, cut it into four thick rings, remove the core, then sprinkle each ring on both sides with sugar and pepper.

3. Preheat the barbecue to medium–high.

4. To make the dressing, mix the ingredients together in a bowl and set aside.

5. Brush the barbecue rack with oil, then place the chicken breasts on the rack. Cook for 10 minutes on each side, or until cooked through. Remove from the heat and leave to rest in a warm place for 4 minutes.

6. Meanwhile, grill the pineapple rings for 2 minutes on each side, or until caramelized.

7. Divide the lettuce between the burger buns and top each with a pineapple ring, chicken breast and spoonful of dressing. Serve immediately.

PER SERVING: 641 KCAL | FAT: 27.6 G | SAT FAT: 9.2 G | CARBS: 56 G | SUGARS: 17.3 G | FIBRE: 4.8 G | PROTEIN: 40.9 G | SALT: 1.9 G

CLASSIC CHICKEN BURGERS

NOTHING BEATS THE SIMPLICITY OF A CLASSIC BREADED CHICKEN BURGER.

 PREP TIME: 25 MINUTES, PLUS CHILLING | COOK TIME: 14 MINUTES | SERVES: 4

4 large skinless, boneless chicken breasts

1 large egg white

1 tbsp cornflour

1 tbsp plain flour

1 egg, beaten

55 g/2 oz fresh breadcrumbs

2 tbsp sunflower oil

4 burger buns, split

4 Little Gem lettuce leaves

2 large tomatoes, sliced

4 tbsp mayonnaise

1. Place each chicken breast between two sheets of clingfilm and beat firmly with a meat mallet or rolling pin to flatten the chicken slightly. Beat together the egg white and cornflour, then brush the mixture over the chicken. Cover and leave to chill for 30 minutes, then coat in the plain flour.

2. Place the egg in a shallow dish and the breadcrumbs in a separate shallow dish. Dip the chicken breasts first in the egg, allowing any excess to drip back into the dish, then in the breadcrumbs, turning to coat.

3. Heat the oil in a heavy-based frying pan over a medium heat. Add the burgers and cook over a medium heat for 6–8 minutes on each side, or until the chicken is tender and cooked through.

4. Serve the burgers in the burger buns with the lettuce leaves, tomato slices and mayonnaise.

PER SERVING: 558 KCAL | FAT: 22.7 G | SAT FAT: 3.6 G | CARBS: 40.7 G | SUGARS: 5.2 G | FIBRE: 4.1 G | PROTEIN: 44.1 G | SALT: 1.3 G

JAPANESE-STYLE CHICKEN PATTIES

THESE FLAVOURSOME BURGERS ARE BEST SERVED WITHOUT A BUN
AND ACCOMPANIED BY A TANGY MANGO SALSA INSTEAD.

 PREP TIME: 15–20 MINUTES, PLUS CHILLING | COOK TIME: 10–15 MINUTES | SERVES: 4

450 g/1 lb fresh chicken mince

1 tbsp grated fresh ginger

1 garlic clove, finely chopped

1 tbsp ketjap manis (Indonesian soy sauce)

½ bunch spring onions, trimmed and finely chopped

2 tbsp vegetable oil

noodle salad (optional)

MANGO SALSA

1 large mango, peeled, stoned and diced

1 red onion, finely chopped

2 ripe tomatoes, finely chopped

1 fresh red jalapeño chilli, deseeded and finely chopped

1 tbsp chopped fresh coriander

2 tbsp lime juice

½ tsp salt (optional)

1. Put the chicken mince, ginger, garlic, ketjap manis and spring onions into a bowl and use your fingertips to combine. Shape the mixture into four patties, transfer to a plate, cover, and let chill for at least 30 minutes.

2. To make the mango salsa, place the ingredients into a small bowl and season with salt, if using, and stir well.

3. Preheat a ridged grill pan over medium heat, then add the oil. Add the patties and cook for 5–6 minutes on each side, until the chicken is thoroughly cooked. Serve immediately with the mango salsa and a simple noodle salad, if using.

PER SERVING: 294 KCAL | FAT: 10.8 G | SAT FAT: 1.6 G | CARBS: 24.5 G | SUGARS: 18.1 G | FIBRE: 3.1 G | PROTEIN: 26.1 G | SALT: 0.4 G

JAMAICAN JERK CHICKEN BURGERS

CHICKEN MINCE IS SPICED UP WITH JAMAICAN JERK SEASONING FOR THESE DELICIOUS BURGERS.

 PREP TIME: 25 MINUTES |  COOK TIME: 20 MINUTES | SERVES: 4

1 tsp soft light brown sugar

1 tsp ground ginger

½ tsp ground allspice

½ tsp dried thyme

½ tsp cayenne pepper

1 tbsp lime juice

2 garlic cloves, finely chopped

450 g/1 lb fresh chicken mince

1 tbsp vegetable oil

1 red pepper, deseeded and cut into large flat pieces

1 tsp olive oil

1 tsp red wine vinegar

4 onion rolls, split

4 Little Gem lettuce leaves

salt and pepper (optional)

1. Place the sugar, ginger, allspice, thyme, cayenne pepper, lime juice, garlic, salt and pepper, if using, into a bowl and mix together. Add the chicken and gently mix to combine. Divide the mixture into four equal-sized portions and shape each portion into a patty.

2. Place a griddle pan over a medium–high heat and add the vegetable oil. Add the red pepper and cook for about 5 minutes, turning frequently, until blackened. Transfer to a bowl, cover with clingfilm or a plate and leave to steam for 5 minutes. Remove the skin and cut the flesh into strips. Toss with the olive oil and vinegar.

3. Put the patties in the pan and cook, covered, for about 5 minutes on each side until brown and cooked through. Place the burgers in the rolls and top with the lettuce and red peppers. Serve immediately.

PER SERVING: 338 KCAL | FAT: 9.8 G | SAT FAT: 1.4 G | CARBS: 30.3 G | SUGARS: 3.7 G | FIBRE: 3.8 G | PROTEIN: 29.8 G | SALT: 1 G

THAI PEANUT CHICKEN BURGERS

THESE JUICY THAI-SPICED BURGERS ARE TOPPED OFF WITH A SWEET AND SPICY PEANUT SAUCE.

 PREP TIME: 30 MINUTES | COOK TIME: 10 MINUTES | SERVES: 4

1 tbsp soft light brown sugar

1 tbsp soy sauce

1 tbsp Thai fish sauce

1 tbsp lemon grass

2 tsp curry powder

1 garlic clove, finely chopped

½ tsp cayenne pepper

450 g/1 lb fresh chicken mince

1 tbsp groundnut oil, for brushing

4 French rolls, split

4 pickled onions, thinly sliced

PEANUT SAUCE

100 g/3½ oz crunchy peanut butter

6 tbsp coconut milk

2 tbsp hot water, plus extra if needed

1 tbsp Thai fish sauce

1 tbsp soft light brown sugar

1 tbsp soy sauce

2 tsp fresh lime juice

1 garlic clove, finely chopped

¼ tsp cayenne pepper

1. Place the sugar, soy sauce, fish sauce, lemon grass, curry powder, garlic and cayenne pepper in a medium-sized bowl, stir to combine, then mix in the chicken. Divide the meat into four equal-sized portions, then use damp hands to shape each portion into a 1-cm/½-inch thick oval patty.

2. To make the peanut sauce, put all of the ingredients into a food processor or blender and process until smooth. Add more water to loosen, if necessary.

3. Lightly brush a griddle pan with the oil and place over a medium–high heat. Add the patties and cook for 5 minutes, then turn and cook for a further 5 minutes until brown and cooked through.

4. Spread both halves of the rolls with the peanut sauce, then top with the burgers and some pickled onions. Serve immediately.

PER SERVING: 507 KCAL | FAT: 25.9 G | SAT FAT: 8 G | CARBS: 35.5 G | SUGARS: 10.4 G | FIBRE: 4.4 G | PROTEIN: 35.1 G | SALT: 4.2 G

CLASSIC TURKEY BURGERS

LOW IN FAT BUT PACKED FULL OF FLAVOUR, TURKEY BURGERS MAKE A DELIGHTFUL CHANGE
FROM THEIR BEEFY COUSINS AND WILL BE POPULAR WITH ALL THE FAMILY.

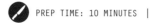 PREP TIME: 10 MINUTES | COOK TIME: 5 MINUTES | SERVES: 4

350 g/12 oz fresh minced turkey breast

4 tbsp fresh wholemeal breadcrumbs

1 small onion, finely chopped

1 apple, peeled, cored and finely chopped

grated rind and juice of 1 small lemon

2 tbsp finely chopped fresh parsley

sunflower oil, for brushing

4 granary rolls or focaccia, split

salt and pepper (optional)

1. Preheat the grill to medium–high and line the grill pan with foil. Place the turkey, breadcrumbs, onion, apple, lemon rind and juice and parsley into a large bowl. Season to taste with salt and pepper, if using, and gently mix to combine. Divide into four equal-sized portions and shape each portion into a patty.

2. Brush the patties with oil and place onto the preheated grill. Cook, turning once, for 5 minutes, or until cooked through. If there are any traces of pink, return to the grill for 1–2 minutes.

3. Place a burger on each bun base, add the bun lids and serve immediately.

PER SERVING: 331 KCAL | FAT: 5.9 G | SAT FAT: 0.8 G | CARBS: 39.9 G | SUGARS: 7.7 G | FIBRE: 4.5 G | PROTEIN: 28.6 G | SALT: 0.8 G

TURKEY & TARRAGON BURGERS

TURKEY AND TARRAGON ADD DISTINCTIVE FLAVOURS TO THESE BURGERS. SERVING ON A BED OF SALAD
INSTEAD OF A BUN MAKES THEM AN EXTRA HEALTHY DINNER OPTION.

 PREP TIME: 20 MINUTES, PLUS CHILLING | COOK TIME: 20–30 MINUTES | SERVES: 4

55 g/2 oz bulgar wheat

1 tsp salt, for cooking the bulgar wheat

450 g/1 lb fresh turkey mince

1 tbsp finely grated orange rind

1 red onion, finely chopped

1 yellow pepper, peeled, deseeded and finely chopped

25 g/1 oz flaked almonds, toasted

1 tbsp chopped fresh tarragon

2 tbsp sunflower oil, for brushing

1 Little Gem lettuce, sliced

4 large tomatoes, quartered

1 red onion, finely sliced

salt and pepper (optional)

1. Bring a medium-sized saucepan of lightly salted water to the boil, add the bulgar wheat and cook for 10–15 minutes, or according to the packet instructions.

2. Drain the bulgar wheat and place in a bowl with the turkey mince, orange rind, onion, yellow pepper, almonds, tarragon, and salt and pepper, if using. Mix together, then shape into four equal-sized burgers. Cover and leave to chill in the refrigerator for 1 hour.

3. Preheat the barbecue to medium–high. Brush the burgers with the oil and cook for 5–6 minutes on each side, or until cooked through.

4. Put a few lettuce leaves, tomato quarters and onion slices on four serving plates and place a burger on top of each. Serve immediately.

PER SERVING: 336 KCAL | FAT: 13.1 G | SAT FAT: 1.5 G | CARBS: 25.8 G | SUGARS: 7.6 G | FIBRE: 6.9 G | PROTEIN: 31.4 G | SALT: 1.8 G

MEXICAN TURKEY BURGERS

THESE SPICY TURKEY BURGERS ARE FILLED WITH GARLIC, JALAPEÑO CHILLIES AND REFRIED BEANS, THEN TOPPED OFF WITH DOLLOPS OF SALSA AND FRESH GUACAMOLE.

 PREP TIME: 25 MINUTES, PLUS CHILLING | COOK TIME: 10–12 MINUTES | SERVES: 4

450 g/1 lb fresh turkey mince

200 g/7 oz canned refried beans

3 garlic cloves, crushed

1 fresh jalapeño chilli, deseeded and finely chopped

2 tbsp tomato purée

1 tbsp chopped fresh coriander

2 tbsp sunflower oil, for brushing

175 g/6 oz baby spinach leaves, shredded

4 cheese-topped burger buns, split

salsa (optional)

tortilla chips, to serve (optional)

salt and pepper (optional)

GUACAMOLE

1 tomato

2 limes

3 small ripe avocados, stoned and peeled

½ onion, finely chopped

¼ tsp ground cumin

¼ tsp mild chilli powder

½ fresh green chilli, such as jalapeño or serrano, deseeded and finely chopped

1. To make the guacamole, place the tomato in a heatproof bowl, pour over boiling water to cover and leave for 30 seconds. Drain and plunge into cold water. Peel off the skin. Cut the tomato in half, deseed and chop the flesh.

2. Squeeze the juice from the limes into a small bowl. Dice the avocados and toss in the bowl of lime juice to prevent the flesh discolouring. Coarsely mash the avocados with a fork.

3. Add the tomato, onion, cumin, chilli powder and chilli to the avocados and mix together. Chill, covered, in the refrigerator until ready to serve.

4. Meanwhile, place the turkey mince in a bowl and break up any large lumps. Beat the refried beans until smooth, then add to the turkey in the bowl.

5. Add the garlic, chilli, tomato purée and coriander with salt and pepper, if using, and mix together. Shape into four equal-sized patties, then cover and leave to chill in the refrigerator for 1 hour.

6. Preheat the barbecue to medium–high. Brush the patties with the oil and cook for 5–6 minutes on each side, or until cooked through.

7. Place the spinach on the bottom halves of the burger buns and top with the burgers. Spoon over a little salsa, if using, and guacamole and top with the lids. Serve immediately with tortilla chips on the side, if liked.

PER SERVING: 589 KCAL | FAT: 26.4 G | SAT FAT: 6.4 G | CARBS: 49 G | SUGARS: 6.5 G | FIBRE: 11 G | PROTEIN: 40.9 G | SALT: 1.8 G

LEMON & MINT TURKEY BURGERS

THE COMBINATION OF LEMON AND MINT GIVES THESE BURGERS A LIGHT, REFRESHING FLAVOUR.

 PREP TIME: 10 MINUTES, PLUS CHILLING | COOK TIME: 15 MINUTES | MAKES: 12

500 g/1 lb 2 oz fresh turkey mince

½ small onion, grated

finely grated rind and juice of 1 lemon

1 garlic clove, finely chopped

2 tbsp finely chopped fresh mint

1 egg, beaten

1 tbsp olive oil

salt and pepper (optional)

12 lemon wedges, to serve

1. Place the turkey, onion, lemon rind and juice, garlic, mint, egg, and salt and pepper, if using, in a bowl and mix well with a fork. Divide into 12 equal-sized portions and shape each portion into a patty. Cover and chill in the refrigerator for at least 1 hour, or overnight.

2. Place the oil in a large, heavy-based frying pan over a medium–high heat. When hot, add the burgers, cooking in batches if necessary. Cook for 4–5 minutes on each side, until golden brown and cooked through.

3. Transfer the burgers to a warmed serving plate and serve immediately with the lemon wedges for squeezing over.

PER SERVING: 69 KCAL | FAT: 2.4 G | SAT FAT: 0.5 G | CARBS: 1.7 G | SUGARS: 0.6 G | FIBRE: 0.2 G | PROTEIN: 10.1 G | SALT: 0.1 G

SESAME TURKEY BURGERS WITH PONZU MAYO

PONZU SAUCE HAS ALL THE RIGHT FLAVOURS ROLLED INTO ONE BOTTLE TO GARNISH THESE DELICIOUS, JUICY BURGERS.

PREP TIME: 20 MINUTES | COOK TIME: 10 MINUTES | SERVES: 4

450 g/1 lb fresh turkey mince

2 tbsp sesame seeds

4 tsp soy sauce

1 tsp toasted sesame oil

1 tsp ground garlic

4 tbsp mayonnaise

2 tbsp ponzu sauce

4 burger buns, split

25 g/1 oz baby lettuce leaves

2 large tomatoes, sliced

½ tsp freshly ground black pepper

2 tbsp soy sauce, to serve

1. Place the turkey in a medium-sized bowl with the sesame seeds, soy sauce, oil and garlic and gently mix to combine. Divide into four equal-sized portions and shape each portion into a patty. Place the patties on a large baking sheet.

2. Preheat the grill to high and place the rack below the heat. Place the patties on the rack and grill for 5 minutes, then turn and continue cooking for a further 4–5 minutes until cooked through.

3. Combine the mayonnaise and ponzu sauce in a small bowl (the mixture will be thin). Coat each cut side of the buns with the sauce, then add the burgers. Top with some lettuce leaves and tomato slices, then sprinkle with pepper and a drizzle of soy sauce. Serve immediately.

PER SERVING: 429 KCAL | FAT: 17.3 G | SAT FAT: 2.6 G | CARBS: 32.6 G | SUGARS: 5.5 G | FIBRE: 3.7 G | PROTEIN: 34 G | SALT: 3.4 G

TURKEY CLUB BURGERS

TAKING A CUE FROM CLUB SANDWICHES, WHICH STACK SLICED TURKEY WITH BACON,
LETTUCE AND TOMATO BETWEEN TOASTED BREAD, THESE BURGERS ARE LAYERED WITH FLAVOUR.

PREP TIME: 20 MINUTES | COOK TIME: 20 MINUTES | SERVES: 4

450 g/1 lb fresh turkey mince

1 garlic clove, finely chopped

½ tsp fresh rosemary

6 bacon rashers

8 white farmhouse bread slices, toasted

3 tbsp ranch-style dressing

4 Little Gem lettuce leaves

2 large tomatoes, sliced

salt and pepper (optional)

1. Preheat the barbecue to medium–high. Combine the turkey mince with the garlic, rosemary and salt and pepper, if using, in a bowl. Divide the mixture into four equal-sized portions and shape each portion into a thick patty.

2. Cook the bacon in a frying pan over a medium heat for about 8 minutes, or until crisp. Drain on kitchen paper and break the pieces in half.

3. Spread each slice of toasted bread with half of the ranch-style dressing.

4. Put the burgers on the rack and cook over a medium heat, covered, for 4–5 minutes on each side, or until cooked through.

5. Place each burger on a slice of bread, add the bacon, lettuce leaves and tomato slices, drizzle with a little more dressing and top with the remaining toasted bread. Serve immediately.

PER SERVING: 493 KCAL | FAT: 14.4 G | SAT FAT: 3.9 G | CARBS: 55.1 G | SUGARS: 10.2 G | FIBRE: 2.7 G | PROTEIN: 34.9 G | SALT: 3.1 G

TURKEY GORGONZOLA BURGERS

LEAVE BLAND TURKEY BURGERS BEHIND WITH THESE DELICIOUS ONES FILLED WITH BLUE CHEESE AND BLACK PEPPER.

PREP TIME: 10 MINUTES | COOK TIME: 10 MINUTES | SERVES: 4

2 shallots, finely chopped

½ tsp salt

½ tsp pepper

55 g/2 oz Gorgonzola cheese or other blue cheese, crumbled

450 g/1 lb fresh turkey mince

4 crusty bread rolls, split

1. Preheat the barbecue to medium–high. Put the shallots, salt, pepper and cheese into a bowl and combine. Add the turkey and gently break up the mince while working all the ingredients together.

2. Divide the mixture into four equal-sized portions and shape each portion into a patty.

3. Place the patties on the rack and cook for about 4 minutes on each side until brown and cooked through. Place the burgers in the buns and serve immediately.

PER SERVING: 399 KCAL | FAT: 6.9 G | SAT FAT: 3.6 G | CARBS: 46.9 G | SUGARS: 3.3 G | FIBRE: 2.4 G | PROTEIN: 35.1 G | SALT: 2.3 G

CHAPTER THREE

VEGGIE & VEGAN

AVOCADO BURGERS WITH QUINOA PATTIES

BURGERS DON'T NEED TO BE UNHEALTHY. HEALTH-BOOSTING AVOCADO ENCASES WELL-SEASONED QUINOA FOR A QUICK AND TASTY SUPERFOOD OPTION.

 PREP TIME: 20 MINUTES, PLUS CHILLING | COOK TIME: 25 MINUTES | SERVES: 4

200 g/7 oz quinoa

1 small onion

1 garlic clove

50 g/1¾ oz drained sun-dried tomatoes in oil

1 egg, beaten

4 avocados

2 tbsp olive oil, for frying

50 g/1¾ oz cream cheese

½ green pepper, deseeded and sliced into rings

1 tbsp poppy seeds

salt and pepper (optional)

1. For the patties, cook the quinoa according to the packet instructions and leave to cool.

2. Place the onion, garlic and sun-dried tomatoes in a food processor and pulse until very finely chopped. Alternatively, finely chop them by hand. Place this mixture in a large mixing bowl, along with the quinoa and egg and season to taste with salt and pepper, if using. Using your hands, mix everything together and shape the mixture into four patties about the size of your palm and 2.5 cm/1 inch thick. Place on a plate and chill in the refrigerator for 30 minutes until firm.

3. Meanwhile, prepare the avocado. Cut the avocado in half around the middle and remove the stone. For the top half of the avocado, being as gentle as possible, make a cut in the top and peel away the skin to reveal the flesh. Repeat for the bottom half and then slice off the base so it can stand.

4. Heat the olive oil in a shallow non-stick frying pan and fry the patties for about 2 minutes on each side until they are golden and crisp.

5. Fill the centre of the avocado with a quinoa patty, cream cheese and a ring of green pepper. Sprinkle poppy seeds over the top and serve.

PER SERVING: 563 KCAL | FAT: 34.9 G | SAT FAT: 7 G | CARBS: 54.4 G | SUGARS: 7.5 G | FIBRE: 14.5 G | PROTEIN: 14.5 G | SALT: 0.2 G

CLASSIC VEGGIE BURGERS

A FANTASTIC BURGER FOR VEGETARIANS AND NON-VEGETARIANS ALIKE, FULL OF FLAVOUR, TEXTURE AND HEALTHY INGREDIENTS.

 PREP TIME: 10 MINUTES, PLUS CHILLING | COOK TIME: 35 MINUTES | SERVES: 4

85 g/3 oz brown rice

400 g/14 oz canned flageolet beans, drained and rinsed

115 g/4 oz unsalted cashew nuts

3 garlic cloves

1 red onion, cut into wedges

115 g/4 oz sweetcorn kernels

2 tbsp tomato purée

1 tbsp chopped fresh oregano

2 tbsp wholemeal flour

2 tbsp sunflower oil

1 Little Gem lettuce, shredded

4 wholemeal buns, split

2 large tomatoes, sliced

4 vegetarian halloumi cheese slices

salt and pepper (optional)

1. Cook the rice in a saucepan of boiling water for 20 minutes, or until tender. Drain and place in a food processor or blender.

2. Add the beans, cashew nuts, garlic, onion, sweetcorn, tomato purée, oregano and salt and pepper, if using, to the rice in the food processor and, using the pulse button, blend together. Shape into four equal-sized patties, then coat in the flour. Cover and leave to chill in the refrigerator for 1 hour.

3. Preheat the barbecue to medium–high. Brush the burgers with the oil and cook for 5–6 minutes on each side, or until cooked through.

4. Place the shredded lettuce leaves on the bottom halves of the buns and top with the burgers. Top each with tomato slices and a halloumi cheese slice. Place under a hot grill for 2 minutes, or until golden brown. Add the bun lids and serve immediately.

PER SERVING: 672 KCAL | FAT: 31.5 G | SAT FAT: 9.3 G | CARBS: 74.4 G | SUGARS: 12.2 G | FIBRE: 12.1 G | PROTEIN: 26.8 G | SALT: 1.4 G

VEGAN BBQ JACKFRUIT BURGER

IT WOULD BE HARD TO TELL FROM FIRST GLANCE THAT THIS ISN'T PULLED PORK. JACKFRUIT BREAKS EASILY INTO SHREDS WITH TWO FORKS AND WITH HOMEMADE BARBECUE SAUCE IT HAS ALL THE FLAVOUR BUT LESS FAT.

PREP TIME: 15 MINUTES | COOK TIME: 15–17 MINUTES | SERVES: 4

280 g/10 oz canned jackfruit, drained

4 vegan wholemeal seeded rolls, split

1 small Little Gem lettuce, leaves separated and torn into pieces

BARBECUE SAUCE

1 tbsp sunflower oil

1 onion, finely chopped

1 dessert apple, cored but not peeled, diced

2 tbsp molasses sugar

2 tbsp cider vinegar

1 tbsp tomato purée

1 tsp dried oregano

2 tsp Dijon mustard

¼ tsp chilli powder

¼ tsp ground allspice (optional)

COLESLAW

175 g/6 oz red cabbage, finely shredded

85 g/3 oz carrot, coarsely grated

juice of ½ unwaxed lemon

2 tbsp freshly chopped coriander or parsley

1. Tip the drained jackfruit onto a chopping board and cut away the central woody core then pull the fruit into thin shreds with two forks.

2. To make the barbecue sauce, heat the oil in a medium saucepan then add the onion and apple, cover and cook over a low heat for 10 minutes, stirring from time to time until the onion and apple have softened. Add the molasses, vinegar, tomato purée, oregano, mustard and chilli powder then the allspice, if using. Mix together and cook for 2–3 minutes, stirring.

3. Add the jackfruit to the barbecue sauce and cook for 3–4 minutes, stirring from time to time until piping hot and well mixed with the sauce.

4. To make the coleslaw, add the cabbage, carrot and lemon juice to a bowl and fork together. Scatter the chopped coriander or parsley over and mix together lightly.

5. Toast each side of the rolls until lightly browned. Transfer to serving plates. Cover the bottom half of each roll with the torn lettuce leaves. Reheat the jackfruit, if needed, then spoon onto the rolls. Add a spoonful of coleslaw to each and cover with the roll tops. Serve immediately.

PER SERVING: 418 KCAL | FAT: 12.1 G | SAT FAT: 0.7 G | CARBS: 67.1 G | SUGARS: 31.7 G | FIBRE: 10.7 G | PROTEIN: 12.1 G | SALT: 0.7 G

CLOUD BREAD BREAKFAST BURGER

CLOUD BREAD IS A FANTASTIC OPTION IF YOU WANT A LOW-CARB MEAL. THESE BURGERS FILLED WITH GUACAMOLE AND CHEESE MAKE A HEARTY BREAKFAST DISH BUT THEY CAN BE SERVED UP ANY TIME OF DAY.

 PREP TIME: 15 MINUTES | 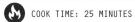 COOK TIME: 25 MINUTES | SERVES: 4

2 tsp extra virgin rapeseed oil

1 large tomato, thickly sliced into four rounds

100 g/3½ oz buffalo mozzarella cheese, drained and sliced into four rounds

CLOUD BREAD ROLLS

8 sprays cooking oil spray

3 large eggs, separated

¾ tsp baking powder

75 g/2¾ oz Greek-style yogurt

1½ tbsp cream cheese

¼ tsp puréed garlic or ready-made garlic paste

¼ tsp salt

25 g/1 oz plain whey protein powder

GUACAMOLE

1 large ripe avocado, peeled and stoned

½ medium–hot red chilli, deseeded and finely chopped

½ small red onion, chopped

juice of ½ lime

15 g/¼ oz chopped fresh coriander

salt and pepper (optional)

1. First make the rolls. Preheat the oven to 150°C/300°F/Gas Mark 2. Line two baking trays with baking parchment and lightly spray with the cooking oil.

2. Put the egg whites into a mixing bowl with the baking powder and whisk with a hand-held electric mixer until they hold stiff peaks. Set aside.

3. Combine the egg yolks in a bowl with the remaining bread roll ingredients, stirring well. Fold the egg whites into the yolk mixture a little at a time – don't over-mix.

4. Using a large spoon, place eight rounds of the egg mixture on the prepared trays, each about the diameter of a burger bun. Bake in the middle of the preheated oven for 20 minutes, or until the rolls are light golden and puffed up. Transfer to wire racks and leave to cool (they will sink a little).

5. To make the guacamole, place the avocado in a bowl with the chilli, red onion, lime juice, coriander leaves and salt and pepper to taste, if using. Mash with a fork, leaving a few small chunks of avocado for texture.

6. To assemble the burgers, spread the flat sides of the cloud rolls with the oil and lightly toast under the grill.

7. Spread the guacamole on the toasted sides of four of the rolls, then add a layer of sliced tomato and top with the cheese rounds. Return them to the grill for a few minutes to melt the cheese, then place the remaining rolls on top to serve.

PER SERVING: 323 KCAL | FAT: 24.3 G | SAT FAT: 8.5 G | CARBS: 9.6 G | SUGARS: 3.1 G | FIBRE: 4 G | PROTEIN: 18.9 G | SALT: 1 G

QUINOA & BEETROOT BURGERS

HERE'S A BURGER WITH A DIFFERENCE. IT WILL BRING A SHADE OF PURPLE
TO YOUR PLATE, BUT IN TRUE BURGER TRADITION IT STILL PROVIDES A TASTY TREAT.

PREP TIME: 35 MINUTES | 1 HOUR 10 MINUTES | SERVES: 8

3–4 small beetroots, peeled and cubed, about 225 g/8 oz in total

135 g/4¾ oz quinoa, rinsed

350 ml/12 fl oz vegetable stock

½ small onion, grated

finely grated rind of ½ lemon

2 tsp cumin seeds

½ tsp salt

¼ tsp pepper

1 large egg white, lightly beaten

10 g/¼ oz quinoa flour, for dusting

1 tbsp vegetable oil, for shallow-frying

8 slices of sourdough toast, to serve

150 g/5½ oz peppery green salad leaves, to serve

WASABI BUTTER

1½ tsp wasabi powder

¾ tsp warm water

70 g/2½ oz butter, at room temperature

1. Cook the beetroots in a steamer for 1 hour.

2. Meanwhile, put the quinoa into a saucepan with the stock. Bring to the boil, then cover and simmer over a very low heat for 10 minutes. Remove from the heat, but leave the pan covered for a further 10 minutes to allow the grains to swell. Fluff up with a fork and spread out on a tray to dry.

3. To make the wasabi butter, mix together the wasabi powder and water. Mix with the butter and chill in the refrigerator.

4. Place the beetroots in a food processor and process until smooth. Tip into a bowl and mix with the quinoa, onion, lemon rind, cumin seeds, salt, pepper and egg white.

5. Divide the mixture into eight equal-sized portions and shape into burgers, each 15 mm/⅝ inch thick, firmly pressing the mixture together. Lightly dust with quinoa flour.

6. Heat a thin layer of oil in a non-stick frying pan. Add the burgers and fry over a medium–high heat, in batches if necessary, for 2 minutes on each side, turning carefully.

7. Place the burgers on the toast and serve with the wasabi butter and salad leaves.

PER SERVING: 281 KCAL | FAT: 11 G | SAT FAT: 5 G | CARBS: 35 G | SUGARS: 5 G | FIBRE: 4 G | PROTEIN: 9 G | SALT 1.3 G

VEGAN SPINACH & LENTIL BURGERS WITH SWEET POTATO BUN

A TASTY BURGER AND BUN RECIPE THAT EVERYONE – NOT JUST VEGANS – WILL ENJOY. SPIRALIZED SWEET POTATO MAKES AN IDEAL LOW CARB REPLACEMENT FOR BREAD.

 PREP TIME: 12 MINUTES, PLUS CHILLING AND SOAKING | COOK TIME: 25 MINUTES | SERVES: 2

BUNS

1 large sweet potato (about 250 g/9 oz)

1 tbsp extra virgin olive oil, plus 2 tsp for brushing

½ tbsp ground chia seeds

1½ tbsp water

salt and pepper (optional)

BURGERS

1 tbsp olive oil

½ small onion, finely chopped

1 garlic clove, crushed

50 g/1¾ oz chestnut mushrooms, finely chopped

½ tbsp ground chia seeds

1½ tbsp water

60 g/2¼ oz ready-washed spinach

90 g/3¼ oz cooked brown lentils

1 tsp red pepper flakes

4 lettuce leaves

salt and pepper (optional)

1. To make the buns, cut the pointed ends off the sweet potato. Spiralize the potato. Add two-thirds of the oil to a frying pan, then add the sweet potato and stir fry over a medium heat for 4–5 minutes until soft. Leave to cool. Meanwhile, put the chia seeds into a small bowl with the water and set aside for 15 minutes.

2. Combine the sweet potato, chia seeds and salt and pepper to taste, if using, in a bowl so that each strand has a coating of the chia mix. Brush four 200-ml/7-fl oz ramekins with oil then divide the sweet potato mixture between them. Press down until the ramekins are approximately 1.5cm–2cm deep with the mix, cover with clingfilm and put a filled jar on top of each ramekin. Leave to stand for 30 minutes.

3. To make the burgers, heat half the oil in a small non-stick frying pan, then add the onion and garlic and sauté over a medium heat, stirring frequently, for 3 minutes until soft. Add the mushrooms and stir for a further 2 minutes. Set aside.

4. Put the chia seeds into a small bowl with the water and set aside for 15 minutes. Cook the spinach for 2 minutes or until just cooked. Squeeze out as much liquid as you can, then chop.

5. Put the lentils in a food processor and pulse for a few seconds, or mash using a pestle and mortar. Transfer to a mixing bowl, add the mushroom mix, spinach, chia seeds, pepper flakes and salt and pepper to taste, if using. Shape into two burgers.

6. Heat the remaining oil in a non-stick frying pan over a medium heat, then carefully add the burgers and fry for about 3 minutes on each side until golden and firm.

7. Meanwhile, heat the remaining oil from the bun recipe in a separate frying pan, add the sweet potato buns and fry over a medium-high heat for 3 minutes on each side or until golden.

8. Serve the burgers inside the sweet potato buns with the lettuce leaves.

PER SERVING: 384 KCAL | FAT: 20.6 G | SAT FAT: 2.6 G | CARBS: 43.5 G | SUGARS: 8 G | FIBRE: 11.8 G | PROTEIN: 9.3 G | SALT: 0.2 G

BEAN BURGERS

RED KIDNEY BEANS AND CHICKPEAS FILL OUT THESE HEARTY VEGETARIAN BURGERS.

 PREP TIME: 15 MINUTES | COOK TIME: 10–12 MINUTES | SERVES: 4

425 g/15 oz canned red kidney beans, drained and rinsed

410 g/14½ oz canned cooked chickpeas, drained and rinsed

1 egg yolk

¼ tsp smoked paprika

50 g/1¾ oz fresh breadcrumbs

3 spring onions, finely chopped

2 tbsp sunflower oil, for brushing

4 crusty bread rolls, split

4 Little Gem lettuce leaves

2 large tomatoes, sliced

4 tbsp soured cream

salt and pepper (optional)

1. Preheat the barbecue to high.

2. Place the beans, chickpeas, egg yolk, paprika, breadcrumbs and spring onions in a large bowl and gently mix to combine. Season to taste with salt and pepper, if using.

3. Divide the mixture into four equal-sized portions and shape each portion into a patty. Season the outside of the patties with salt and pepper, if using, and lightly brush with oil.

4. Oil the barbecue rack. Cook the burgers for 5 minutes on each side, or until cooked through. Brush the inside of the buns with oil and toast over the barbecue, cut-side down, for 1–2 minutes.

5. Place the lettuce and tomatoes on each bun base, then top with the burgers and soured cream. Add the bun lids and serve immediately.

PER SERVING: 496 KCAL | FAT: 12.9 G | SAT FAT: 2.6 G | CARBS: 72 G | SUGARS: 6.3 G | FIBRE: 12 G | PROTEIN: 18.6 G | SALT: 0.9 G

VEGAN KALE & BLACK BEAN SLOPPY JOE

BEING VEGAN DOESN'T MEAN MISSING OUT. THIS MEAT-LESS VERSION OF A CLASSIC IS JUST AS DELICIOUS AND FILLING AS THE ORIGINAL.

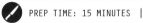 PREP TIME: 15 MINUTES | COOK TIME: 40 MINUTES | SERVES: 4

2 sweet potatoes, cut into 8 wedges

4 tbsp olive oil

½ tsp salt

½ tsp pepper

2 avocados, peeled, stoned and sliced

4 vegan burger buns, split

SLOPPY JOE

2 tbsp olive oil

2 garlic cloves, crushed

¼ tsp chilli flakes

1 tsp cumin powder

1 tsp coriander powder

1 tsp mild paprika

½ tsp dried oregano

1 tbsp light brown sugar

150 g/5 oz canned chopped tomatoes

40 g/1½ oz kale, cored and shredded

70g/2½ oz canned black beans, drained

salt and pepper (optional)

1. Preheat the oven to 180°C/350°F/Gas Mark 4.

2. Place the potatoes in a bowl and add the oil, salt and pepper. Toss well to coat. Arrange the potatoes in a single layer on a non-stick tray and bake in the oven for 25–30 minutes, until golden brown and tender.

3. Meanwhile, to make the sloppy joe, heat the oil in a medium-sized saucepan over a low heat and add the garlic and chilli flakes. Gently cook until the garlic starts to turn golden. Add the spices and salt and pepper, if using. Stir for a few seconds, then add the sugar, chopped tomatoes and kale. Cook for 5 minutes, or until the kale has wilted. Add the black beans and cook for a further minute.

4. Toast the burger buns and place two slices of avocado and two potato wedges on each bun base. Spoon the kale and black bean sloppy joe on top.

5. Add the bun lids and serve immediately.

PER SERVING: 550 KCAL | FAT: 33.1 G | SAT FAT: 4.7 G | CARBS: 54.4 G | SUGARS: 11 G | FIBRE: 10.7 G | PROTEIN: 10.6 G | SALT: 1.4 G

SWEET POTATO & HALLOUMI BURGERS

THERE ARE SO MANY INTERESTING TEXTURES AND FLAVOURS VYING FOR YOUR ATTENTION IN THESE TASTY VEGETARIAN BURGERS THAT A BUN ISN'T REQUIRED.

 PREP TIME: 20 MINS, PLUS CHILLING | COOK TIME: 40–50 MINUTES | SERVES: 4

450 g/1 lb sweet potatoes, cut into chunks

175 g/6 oz broccoli florets, cut into small pieces

2 garlic cloves, crushed

1 red onion, finely chopped or grated

1½ fresh red jalapeño chillies, deseeded and finely chopped

175 g/6 oz vegetarian halloumi cheese, grated

2 tbsp wholemeal flour

2 tbsp sunflower oil

450 g/1 lb onions, sliced

1 tbsp chopped fresh coriander

salt and pepper (optional)

1. Add a little salt, if using, to a saucepan of water and bring to the boil. Add the sweet potato and cook for 15–20 minutes, or until tender. Drain and mash. Bring a separate saucepan of water to the boil, add the broccoli and cook for 3 minutes, then drain and plunge into cold water. Drain again, then add to the mashed sweet potato.

2. Stir in the garlic, red onion, chilli, halloumi cheese, and salt and pepper to taste, if using. Mix well and shape into four equal-sized patties, then coat in the flour. Cover and chill in the refrigerator for at least 1 hour.

3. Heat 1½ tablespoons of the oil in a heavy-based frying pan. Add the onions and fry over a medium heat for 12–15 minutes, or until soft. Stir in the coriander and set aside.

4. Place the burgers in the pan, adding more oil if necessary. Cook over a medium heat for 5–6 minutes on each side, or until they are cooked through.

5. Top the burgers with the fried onions and coriander and serve.

PER SERVING: 396 KCAL | FAT: 18.7 G | SAT FAT: 8.7 G | CARBS: 44.1 G | SUGARS: 12.9 G | FIBRE: 7.6 G | PROTEIN: 15.6 G | SALT: 1.3 G

VEGAN TOFU BURGERS WITH CORIANDER AÏOLI

TOFU IS AN EXCELLENT SOURCE OF PROTEIN AND IS IDEAL FOR VEGETARIANS, VEGANS AND MEAT-EATERS ALIKE.

 PREP TIME: 15 MINUTES, PLUS MARINATING | COOK TIME: 6 MINUTES | SERVES: 3

280 g/10 oz firm tofu

2 tbsp soy sauce

½ tsp vegan Worcestershire sauce

1 garlic clove, finely chopped

¼ tsp red pepper flakes

8 small fresh coriander sprigs, roughly chopped

50 ml/2 fl oz vegan mayonnaise

3 vegan burger buns, split

½ small red onion, thinly sliced

3 Little Gem lettuce leaves

1. Preheat the grill to high and place the rack about 15 cm/6 inches below the heat. Line the grill pan with foil.

2. Drain the tofu and pat dry. Slice into 1-cm/½-inch thick slabs that will roughly fit in the buns and drain on kitchen paper.

3. Combine the soy sauce, Worcestershire sauce, half the garlic and the red pepper flakes in a shallow dish wide enough to fit the tofu in a single layer. Place the tofu in the mixture, then turn to coat on both sides. Place in the refrigerator and marinate for at least 15 minutes or for up to 3 hours.

4. Put the coriander and the remaining garlic into a small food processor or blender and purée. Add the mayonnaise and mix until smooth.

5. Transfer the tofu to the prepared pan. Cook under the preheated grill for 3 minutes on each side, or until brown.

6. Spread the coriander aïoli on both halves of the buns, then add one third of the tofu to each of the bun bases. Add the onion and lettuce, finish with the top halves of the buns and serve immediately.

PER SERVING: 321 KCAL | FAT: 14.8 G | SAT FAT: 2.2 G | CARBS: 33.4 G | SUGARS: 4.9 G | FIBRE: 3.2 G | PROTEIN: 15.2 G | SALT: 2.2 G

PORTOBELLO MUSHROOM BURGERS WITH MOZZARELLA

THIS VEGETARIAN BURGER COMBINES MARINATED PORTOBELLO MUSHROOMS WITH MOZZARELLA CHEESE AND PESTO IN A FOCACCIA 'BUN'.

PREP TIME: 10 MINUTES | COOK TIME: 15 MINUTES | SERVES: 4

4 tsp olive oil

2 tsp red wine vinegar

1 garlic clove, finely chopped

4 large Portobello mushrooms, caps only

8 slices fresh vegetarian mozzarella-style cheese

4 x 15-cm/6-inch square pieces focaccia, split

50 ml/2 fl oz vegetarian basil pesto

2 large tomatoes, sliced

baby rocket leaves (optional)

salt and pepper (optional)

1. Preheat the grill to high and the oven to 160°C/325°F/Gas Mark 3. Whisk together the oil, vinegar and garlic in a medium-sized bowl. Place the mushrooms gill side-up on a baking tray, then drizzle with the vinaigrette and season to taste with salt and pepper, if using.

2. Place under the preheated grill and cook for about 5–8 minutes until the mushrooms are tender. Place the cheese slices on top and cook for a further 1–2 minutes until bubbling. Meanwhile, put the focaccia on a lower rack in the preheated oven for 5 minutes to warm through.

3. Lightly spread the focaccia with the pesto, then add the mushrooms. Top with the tomato slices and rocket, if using. Serve immediately.

PER SERVING: 501 KCAL | FAT: 27.7 G | SAT FAT: 8.3 G | CARBS: 41 G | SUGARS: 4.7 G | FIBRE: 3.6 G | PROTEIN: 22.6 G | SALT: 2.4 G

VEGAN BENTO BURGERS

THESE JAPANESE VEGAN SNACKS ARE MADE WITH COOKED RICE PRESSED
INTO THE SHAPE OF BUNS, CRISP ON THE OUTSIDE, WITH SAVOURY SPINACH INSIDE.

 PREP TIME: 15 MINUTES, PLUS RESTING | COOK TIME: 15 MINUTES | SERVES: 5

8 shiitake mushrooms, stalks removed

450 g/1 lb washed spinach leaves

2 tbsp soy sauce

2 tbsp mirin

2 tsp sesame seeds, toasted

1 tsp salt

225 ml/8 fl oz lukewarm water

425 g/15 oz short- or medium-grain white rice, rinsed and cooked and kept warm

2 tsp sesame oil, for frying

1. Preheat the grill to high. Arrange the mushrooms on the grill pan and cook for 3 minutes on each side until brown and tender. Thinly slice the mushrooms and place in a medium-sized bowl.

2. Bring a large saucepan of water to the boil. Add the spinach and blanch for 1 minute. Drain, cool under cold running water, then squeeze dry. Add the mushrooms to the spinach, then add the soy sauce, mirin and sesame seeds and combine.

3. Dissolve the salt in the warm water. Place the rice in a wide bowl and divide into ten equal-sized portions. Wet your hands with the water and very firmly press each portion into a rice bun. Wet your hands each time you make a bun. Leave to set for 20 minutes.

4. Place a non-stick frying pan or ridged griddle pan over a medium heat and lightly coat the base with oil. Add the buns and cook for 4 minutes on each side (turning very gently) until brown.

5. Put the spinach mixture on top of half the rice buns, then top with the remaining buns. Wrap the burgers in squares of baking paper to hold them together prior to serving and serve within 2 hours.

PER SERVING: 375 KCAL | FAT: 3.4 G | SAT FAT: 0.5 G | CARBS: 74.8 G | SUGARS: 2.9 G | FIBRE: 3.6 G | PROTEIN: 9.4 G | SALT: 2.3 G

VEGGIE BURGER BOWL

THESE BURGERS ARE FILLING AND NUTRITIOUS. YOU COULD EAT THEM IN A BUN, BUT SERVING THEM
IN A BOWL ON A BED OF COLOURFUL ROASTED RATATOUILLE IS EVEN BETTER.

 PREP TIME: 25 MINUTES, PLUS 20 MINUTES CHILLING | COOK TIME: 35–40 MINUTES | SERVES: 4

2 red peppers, deseeded and chopped

2 yellow peppers, deseeded and chopped

2 red onions, cut into wedges

2 courgettes, thickly sliced

3 tbsp olive oil

400 g/14 oz canned chickpeas, drained and rinsed

200 g/7 oz frozen peas, thawed

200 g/7 oz frozen sweetcorn, thawed

10 g/¼ oz fresh coriander (including stalks)

¼ tsp ground cumin

80 g/2¾ oz plain flour

1 tbsp sunflower seeds

1 tbsp sesame seeds

salt and pepper (optional)

DRESSING

1 avocado, peeled, stoned and chopped

200 g/7 oz natural yogurt

2 spring onions, chopped

1 garlic clove, crushed

1 tbsp lime juice

salt and pepper (optional)

1. Preheat the oven to 200°C/400°F/Gas Mark 6.

2. Place the red peppers, yellow peppers, onions and courgettes in a roasting tin and drizzle with 1 tablespoon of the oil. Roast for 35–40 minutes, until they are slightly charred at the edges.

3. Meanwhile, place the chickpeas, peas, sweetcorn, coriander, the cumin and 70 g/2½ oz of the flour in a food processor and process to a thick paste. Add the sunflower seeds and sesame seeds, season with salt and pepper, if using, and process again to mix together.

4. Using wet hands, divide the mixture into four portions and shape each portion into a patty. Dust the patties with the remaining flour and chill in the refrigerator for 20 minutes.

5. Meanwhile to make the dressing, place the avocado, yogurt, spring onions, garlic and lime juice in a small blender and blend until smooth. Season to taste with salt and pepper, if using.

6. Heat the remaining oil in a frying pan, add the burgers and cook for 5–6 minutes on each side, until cooked through.

7. Divide the roasted ratatouille between four bowls, top each portion with a burger, then drizzle with the dressing and serve immediately.

PER SERVING: 534 KCAL | FAT: 24 G | SAT FAT: 4 G | CARBS: 66 G | SUGARS: 18.6 G | FIBRE: 15.8 G | PROTEIN: 16.9 G | SALT: 0.1 G

BEETROOT, COURGETTE & CARROT BURGERS

THE TANGY YOGURT SAUCE CONTRASTS WITH THE SWEET, EARTHY VEGETABLES IN THESE THESE WHOLESOME, CRISP BURGERS.

 PREP TIME: 30 MINUTES, PLUS STANDING AND CHILLING | COOK TIME: 35–40 MINUTES | SERVES: 5

100 g/3½ oz millet

175 ml/6 fl oz lightly salted water

150 g/5½ oz raw beetroot, grated

30 g/1 oz carrots, grated

175 g/6 oz courgettes, grated

60 g/2¼ oz walnuts, finely chopped

2 tbsp cider vinegar

2 tbsp extra virgin olive oil, plus extra for frying

1 egg, beaten

2 tbsp cornflour

5 multi-grain buns, split

5 Little Gem lettuce leaves

salt and pepper (optional)

YOGURT SAUCE

225 ml/8 fl oz natural yogurt

2 tsp finely chopped garlic

salt and pepper (optional)

1. Rinse and drain the millet and place in a small saucepan with the salted water. Place over a medium heat, bring to a simmer, cover and cook over a very low heat for 20–25 minutes until tender. Remove from the heat and leave to stand for 5 minutes, covered.

2. Put the beetroot, carrots, courgettes and walnuts into a large bowl. Add the millet, vinegar, oil, salt and pepper, if using, and mix well. Add the egg and cornflour, mix again, then chill in the refrigerator for 2 hours.

3. To make the sauce, put the yogurt in a fine strainer over a bowl and drain for at least 30 minutes. Stir in the garlic and season to taste with salt and pepper, if using.

4. Pack the beetroot mixture into a 125 ml/4 fl oz cup, then shape into a patty. Repeat to make a total of five burgers. Place a ridged griddle pan or large frying pan over a medium heat and coat with oil. Add the patties and cook for about 5 minutes on each side, turning carefully, until brown.

5. Spread the buns with the yogurt sauce and place the burgers in the buns, topped with the lettuce. Serve immediately.

PER SERVING: 471 KCAL | FAT: 20.5 G | SAT FAT: 3.5 G | CARBS: 59.3 G | SUGARS: 8.8 G | FIBRE: 6.2 G | PROTEIN: 15 G | SALT: 0.9 G

VEGAN BUTTERNUT SQUASH & POLENTA BURGERS

THE THICK AND CREAMY POLENTA IS A FANTASTIC ADDITION TO THESE VEGAN BURGERS.

 PREP TIME: 20 MINUTES, PLUS CHILLING | COOK TIME: 40 MINUTES | SERVES: 4

450 g/1 lb butternut squash, peeled, deseeded and chopped

150 ml/5 fl oz water

85 g /3 oz quick-cook polenta

115 g/4 oz celeriac, peeled and grated

6 spring onions, finely chopped

115 g/4 oz pecan nuts, chopped

2 tbsp chopped fresh mixed herbs

2 tbsp wholemeal flour

1 tbsp sunflower oil, for oiling

4 vegan burger buns, split and toasted

2 large tomatoes, sliced

watercress (optional)

salt and pepper (optional)

1. Bring a large saucepan of water to the boil, add the butternut squash, bring back to the boil and cook for 15–20 minutes, or until tender. Drain and finely chop or mash. Place the 150 ml/5 fl oz of water in a separate saucepan and bring to the boil. Slowly pour in the polenta in a steady stream and cook over a low heat, stirring constantly, for 5 minutes, or until thick.

2. Remove the pan from the heat and stir in the squash, celeriac, spring onions, nuts, herbs and salt and pepper, if using. Mix well, then shape into four equal-sized burgers. Coat the burgers in the flour, cover and chill in the refrigerator for 1 hour. Meanwhile, preheat the barbecue to medium–high.

3. Oil the barbecue rack. Lightly brush the burgers with oil and cook for 5–6 minutes on each side, or until cooked through. Transfer to serving plates and serve immediately in the burger buns topped with tomato slices and watercress, if using.

PER SERVING: 558 KCAL | FAT: 28.1 G | SAT FAT: 2.8 G | CARBS: 69.4 G | SUGARS: 8.4 G | FIBRE: 9.6 G | PROTEIN: 12.5 G | SALT: 0.6 G

GREENS, PEAS & BEANS BURGERS

A MIXTURE OF PEPPERY GREENS ADDS COLOUR AND NUTRIENTS TO THESE MOUTH-WATERING VEGGIE BURGERS. THEY ARE LIGHT YET VERY FLAVOURFUL – EVEN MEAT-EATERS WILL GOBBLE THEM UP.

 PREP TIME: 30 MINUTES, PLUS STANDING | COOK TIME: 10 MINUTES | SERVES: 8

115 g/4 oz peppery salad leaves, such as rocket, mustard greens, pak choi (green part only) or a mixture, thick stems removed

60 g/2¼ oz cooked peas, mashed

400 g/14 oz canned butter beans, drained, rinsed and mashed

1 tbsp grated onion

1½ tbsp chopped fresh mint

1 egg, beaten

40 g/1½ oz stale breadcrumbs

3 tbsp vegetable oil

4 wholemeal pittas, halved crossways

16 cherry tomatoes, halved

8 tbsp mayonnaise

salt and pepper (optional)

1. Roughly slice the salad leaves. Steam for 3 minutes, then drain and rinse under cold running water, squeezing out as much liquid as possible.

2. Combine the cooked greens with the peas, beans, onion, mint, egg and salt and pepper, if using. Mix thoroughly with a fork. Stir in the breadcrumbs, mixing well. Leave to stand at room temperature for 30 minutes.

3. Divide the mixture into eight 1-cm/½-inch thick patties, each 6 cm/2½ inches in diameter, firming the edges well.

4. Heat the oil in a non-stick frying pan over a medium–high heat. Working in batches, add the patties and fry for 2½–3 minutes on each side, turning carefully, until golden and crisp. Meanwhile, preheat the grill to medium.

5. Toast the pitta halves under the preheated grill. Stuff each half with a bean patty, cherry tomato halves and a dollop of mayonnaise. Serve immediately.

PER SERVING: 294 KCAL | FAT: 17 G | SAT FAT: 2.4 G | CARBS: 28.4 G | SUGARS: 3 G | FIBRE: 5 G | PROTEIN: 7.6 G | SALT: 0.7 G

VEGAN SMOKY MUSHROOM & CORIANDER BURGERS

THE SMOKINESS OF THE PAPRIKA COMPLIMENTS THE MUSHROOMS AND RED KIDNEY BEANS PERFECTLY.

 PREP TIME: 15 MINUTES | 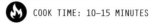 COOK TIME: 10–15 MINUTES | SERVES: 6

425 g/15 oz canned red kidney beans, drained and rinsed

2 tbsp sunflower oil, for frying

1 onion, finely chopped

115 g/4 oz mushrooms, finely chopped

1 large carrot, coarsely grated

2 tsp smoked paprika

70 g/2½ oz porridge oats

3 tbsp dark soy sauce

2 tbsp tomato purée

30 g/1 oz fresh coriander, including stalks, chopped

3 tbsp plain flour

3 tbsp sunflower oil, for brushing

6 Little Gem lettuce leaves

6 vegan burger buns, split

1 avocado, peeled, stoned and sliced (optional)

tomato salsa (optional)

salt and pepper (optional)

1. Place the beans in a large bowl and mash as thoroughly as you can with a potato masher. Heat the oil in a frying pan, add the onion and fry for 2 minutes, until translucent. Add the mushrooms, carrot and paprika and fry for a further 4 minutes, until the vegetables are soft.

2. Add the fried vegetables to the beans with the oats, soy sauce, tomato purée and coriander. Season with salt and pepper, if using, and mix well. Divide into six equal portions and shape into burgers, then turn in the flour to coat lightly.

3. Preheat a griddle pan until smoking. Lightly brush the tops of the burgers with oil, then place oiled side down on the pan. Cook over a medium heat for 2–3 minutes, until lightly charred underneath. Lightly brush the tops with oil, turn and cook for a further 2-3 minutes on the other side.

4. Place lettuce on the base of each bun, top with a burger, some avocado slices, tomato salsa, if using, and the bun lid. Serve immediately.

PER SERVING: 390 KCAL | FAT: 15.9 G | SAT FAT: 1.9 G | CARBS: 49.7 G | SUGARS: 6 G | FIBRE: 7.3 G | PROTEIN: 12.1 G | SALT: 1.7 G

LENTIL BURGERS

THE WHOLE FAMILY – WHETHER VEGETARIAN OR NOT – WILL ENJOY THESE BURGERS MADE FROM TASTY PUY LENTILS THREADED THROUGH WITH DEEP GREEN SPINACH.

 PREP TIME: 20 MINUTES | COOK TIME: 25 MINUTES | SERVES: 4

100 g/3½ oz floury potatoes, cut into 2-cm/¾-inch cubes

100 g/3½ oz baby spinach leaves

250 g/9 oz cooked Puy lentils

1 onion, roughly chopped

100 g/3½ oz chestnut mushrooms, roughly chopped

1 heaped tbsp chopped fresh parsley

2 tsp fresh thyme leaves

1 small egg, beaten

1½ tbsp extra virgin rapeseed oil

4 wholemeal burger buns, split

40 g/1½ oz light mayonnaise

2 large tomatoes, sliced

240 g/8½ oz mixed salad leaves

salt and pepper (optional)

1. Bring a small saucepan of water to the boil. Add the potatoes, bring back to the boil and cook for 10 minutes, until soft. Drain thoroughly, then return to the hob with the heat turned off. The residual heat will dry out any remaining moisture – shake the pan to help.

2. Meanwhile, put the spinach in a microwaveable bowl and microwave on High (850 watts) for 1½ minutes, or until thoroughly wilted. Transfer to a sieve and push all the moisture out using the end of a rolling pin or a pestle. Dry again on strong kitchen paper.

3. Put the potatoes, lentils, onion, mushrooms, 1 teaspoon of salt, and pepper, if using, in a food processor and process for 1 minute to a semi-smooth mixture with some texture. Stir the spinach, parsley and thyme into the mixture by hand, then stir in the egg. Shape into four large 1-cm/½-inch thick burgers.

4. Heat the oil in a large, non-stick frying pan. Add the burgers and cook, in batches if necessary, over a medium heat for 3 minutes on each side. You may need to reduce the heat to low for the last minute of cooking on either side to prevent the burgers from over-browning.

5. Spread the burger buns with the mayonnaise. Place the burgers in the buns with the tomato slices and serve immediately with the salad leaves on the side.

PER SERVING: 363 KCAL | FAT: 12.6 G | SAT FAT: 2.1 G | CARBS: 47.5 G | SUGARS: 4.4 G | FIBRE: 11.2 G | PROTEIN: 18 G | SALT: 2.2 G

VEGAN CHICKPEA WALNUT PATTIES

THESE HEARTY PATTIES ARE VERY SIMILAR TO FALAFEL, BUT HAVE THE ADDED RICHNESS AND FLAVOUR OF WALNUTS.

 PREP TIME: 20 MINUTES, PLUS CHILLING | COOK TIME: 10 MINUTES | SERVES: 4

2 garlic cloves

1 shallot

425 g/15 oz canned chickpeas, drained and rinsed

15 g/½ oz fresh flat-leaf parsley

1 tsp ground coriander

1 tsp ground cumin

½ tsp salt

¾ tsp cayenne pepper

2 tbsp olive oil

2 tbsp plain flour

½ tsp baking powder

60 g/2¼ oz roasted, unsalted walnuts

2 tbsp sunflower oil, for frying

4 sesame seed burger buns, split

4 Little Gem lettuce leaves

2 large tomatoes, sliced

4 tbsp vegan mayonnaise (optional)

1. Put the garlic and shallot into a food processor and pulse to chop. Add the chickpeas, parsley, coriander, cumin, salt, cayenne pepper, olive oil and flour and pulse to a chunky purée. Add the baking powder and pulse once to incorporate. Add the walnuts and pulse once to incorporate.

2. Shape the chickpea mixture into four equal-sized patties, about 10 cm/4 inches in diameter. Chill in the refrigerator for at least 30 minutes or overnight.

3. Heat the sunflower oil in a large frying pan over a medium–high heat. Add the patties and cook for 4–5 minutes on each side until golden brown.

4. Serve hot layered in the bun with lettuce, tomato slices and vegan mayonnaise, if using.

PER SERVING: 320 KCAL | FAT: 24.7 G | SAT FAT: 2.6 G | CARBS: 18.1 G | SUGARS: 3.5 G | FIBRE: 5.2 G | PROTEIN: 7 G | SALT: 0.9 G

VEGAN MUSHROOM, SPINACH & RICE BURGERS

MADE WITH BROWN RICE, BEANS AND VEGETABLES, THESE HEALTHY VEGAN BURGERS ARE SATISFYING AND DELICIOUS, SERVED ATOP LARGE FIELD MUSHROOMS.

 PREP TIME: 20 MINUTES, PLUS CHILLING | COOK TIME: 50 MINUTES | SERVES: 4

25 g/1 oz brown rice

4 tbsp olive oil

3 garlic cloves, crushed

300 g/10½ oz button mushrooms, chopped

175 g/6 oz fresh spinach leaves

300 g/10½ oz canned borlotti beans, drained and rinsed

1 medium orange pepper, deseeded, peeled and finely chopped

55 g/2 oz flaked almonds

2 tbsp chopped fresh basil

55 g/2 oz wholemeal breadcrumbs

2 tbsp wholemeal flour

2 large tomatoes, sliced

4 large field mushrooms

salt and pepper (optional)

1. Cook the rice in a saucepan of boiling water for 20–25 minutes, or until tender. Drain and place in a food processor.

2. Heat 1 tablespoon of the oil in a frying pan. Add the garlic and button mushrooms and cook for 5 minutes. Add to the rice in the food processor.

3. Reserve 25 g/1 oz of the spinach leaves. Add the remaining spinach, the beans, orange pepper, almonds, basil, breadcrumbs, salt and pepper, if using, to the rice mixture in the food processor and pulse to finely chop. Mix well, then shape into four equal-sized burgers. Coat in the flour, then cover and chill in the refrigerator for 1 hour.

4. Preheat the grill to medium–high. Heat 2 tablespoons of the oil in a non-stick frying pan, add the burgers and cook for 5–6 minutes each side, or until golden and cooked through. Meanwhile, brush the tomato slices and field mushrooms with the remaining oil and grill for 6–8 minutes, turning once, until soft.

5. Place the reserved spinach leaves on individual serving plates and top each with a mushroom. Add a burger and tomato slice and serve immediately.

PER SERVING: 378 KCAL | FAT: 22.3 G | SAT FAT: 2.6 G | CARBS: 32.7 G | SUGARS: 7.3 G | FIBRE: 10 G | PROTEIN: 14.5 G | SALT: 0.2 G

POTATO, BLUE CHEESE & APPLE BURGERS

THE SWEETNESS OF THE APPLE COMPLIMENTS THE STRONG FLAVOUR OF THE BLUE CHEESE TO CREATE A UNIQUE AND APPETIZING BURGER.

 PREP TIME: 12 MINUTES, PLUS CHILLING | COOK TIME: 25–35 MINUTES | SERVES: 4

175 g/6 oz new potatoes

225 g/8 oz mixed nuts, such as pecans, almonds and hazelnuts

1 onion, roughly chopped

2 small apples, peeled, cored and grated

175 g/6 oz vegetarian blue cheese, such as Stilton, crumbled

55 g/2 oz fresh wholemeal breadcrumbs

2 tbsp wholemeal flour

2 tbsp sunflower oil, for brushing

baby lettuce leaves (optional)

4 cheese-topped burger buns, split

½ red onion, thinly sliced

salt and pepper (optional)

1. Cook the potatoes in a saucepan of boiling water for 15–20 minutes, or until tender. Drain and, using a potato masher, crush into small pieces. Place in a large bowl.

2. Place the nuts and onion in a food processor or blender and, using the pulse button, chop finely. Add the nuts, onion, apple, cheese and breadcrumbs to the potatoes in the bowl. Season to taste with salt and pepper, if using. Mix well, then shape into four equal-sized patties. Coat in the flour, then cover and leave to chill in the refrigerator for 1 hour.

3. Preheat the barbecue to medium–high. Brush the burgers with the oil and cook for 5–6 minutes on each side, or until cooked through.

4. Place the lettuce leaves on the bottom halves of the buns, if using, and top with the burgers. Add some red onion slices, add the lids and serve immediately.

PER SERVING: 948 KCAL | FAT: 69.1 G | SAT FAT: 17.9 G | CARBS: 61.5 G | SUGARS: 12.3 G | FIBRE: 9.9 G | PROTEIN: 27.9 G | SALT: 1.7 G

VEGAN FALAFEL BURGERS

FALAFEL BURGERS MAKE AN EASY, HEALTHY LUNCH OR DINNER ANY DAY OF THE WEEK, ANY TIME OF YEAR.

PREP TIME: 15 MINUTES | COOK TIME: 4 MINUTES | SERVES: 4

800 g/1 lb 12 oz canned chickpeas, drained and rinsed

1 small onion, chopped

juice and grated rind of 1 unwaxed lime

2 tsp ground coriander

2 tsp ground cumin

6 tbsp plain flour

4 tbsp olive oil

30 g/1 oz fresh watercress sprigs

ready-made vegan tomato salsa, (optional)

1. Put the chickpeas, onion, lime juice and rind and the spices into a food processor and process to a coarse paste.

2. Tip out onto a clean work surface and shape into four equal-sized patties.

3. Spread out the flour on a large flat plate and turn the patties in it to coat.

4. Heat the oil in a large frying pan, add the patties and cook for 2 minutes on each side, until crisp.

5. Serve immediately with the watercress and tomato salsa, if using.

PER SERVING: 334 KCAL | FAT: 16.3 G | SAT FAT: 2 G | CARBS: 34.6 G | SUGARS: 6.9 G | FIBRE: 8.8 G | PROTEIN: 9.7 G | TRACE SALT

VEGETARIAN CHILLI BURGERS

YOU CAN MAKE THESE VEGGIE BURGERS AS SPICY AS YOU LIKE BY ADDING JALAPEÑOS TO TASTE.

 PREP TIME: 25 MINUTES, PLUS CHILLING | COOK TIME: 20 MINUTES | SERVES: 4

85 g /3 oz bulgar wheat

300 g/10½ oz canned red kidney beans, drained and rinsed

300 g /10½ oz canned cannellini beans, drained and rinsed

1 fresh jalapeño chilli, deseeded and roughly chopped

2 garlic cloves, roughly chopped

6 spring onions, roughly chopped

1 yellow pepper, peeled, deseeded and chopped

1 tbsp chopped fresh coriander,

115 g/4 oz grated vegetarian Cheddar cheese

2 tbsp wholemeal flour

2 tbsp sunflower oil

1 large tomato, sliced

4 wholemeal buns, split

salt and pepper (optional)

1. Place the bulgar wheat in a sieve and rinse under cold running water. Add the bulgar wheat to a saucepan of water and cook for 12 minutes, or until tender. Drain and reserve.

2. Place the beans in a food processor with the chilli, garlic, spring onions, yellow pepper, coriander and half the cheese. Using the pulse button, chop finely. Add to the cooked bulgar wheat with salt and pepper, if using. Mix well, then shape into four equal-sized burgers. Cover and chill in the refrigerator for 1 hour.

3. Coat the burgers in the flour. Preheat the grill to medium. Heat a heavy-based frying pan and add the oil. When hot, add the burgers and cook over a medium heat for 5–6 minutes on each side, or until piping hot.

4. Place two slices of tomato on top of each burger and sprinkle with the remaining cheese. Cook under the hot grill for 2–3 minutes, or until the cheese begins to melt. Serve in the wholemeal buns.

PER SERVING: 536 KCAL | FAT: 19.9 G | SAT FAT: 6.8 G | CARBS: 64.4 G | SUGARS: 7.2 G | FIBRE: 14.1 G | PROTEIN: 24.2 G | SALT: 1.1 G

CHAPTER FOUR

FISH

SALMON QUINOA BURGERS

MADE WITH SALMON, QUINOA AND EGG, THESE BURGERS ARE FULL OF PROTEIN. TOPPED WITH
SPICY MAYONNAISE AND A SPRITZ OF LIME JUICE, YOU'LL BE HARD-PRESSED TO FIND A TASTIER BURGER.

 PREP TIME: 15 MINUTES, PLUS CHILLING | COOK TIME: 20–25 MINUTES | SERVES: 4

125 g/4½ oz quinoa

275 g/9¾ oz cooked salmon, broken into flakes

1 egg, beaten

4 spring onions, trimmed and sliced

1 tbsp chopped fresh coriander

4 wholemeal burger buns, split

1 tbsp olive oil, for frying

30 g/1 oz fresh watercress sprigs

¼ cucumber, sliced

salt and pepper (optional)

4 lime wedges, to serve

SPICY MAYONNAISE

2 tbsp capers, chopped

4 tbsp mayonnaise

juice of ½ lime

1. Bring a large saucepan of water to the boil. Add the quinoa and boil for 8–10 minutes. Drain well.

2. Place the quinoa in a bowl with the salmon, egg, spring onions and coriander. Season to taste with salt and pepper, if using, and mix well.

3. With your hands, shape the mixture into four patties. Place them on a plate and chill in the refrigerator for 20 minutes.

4. Meanwhile, make the spicy mayonnaise. Mix the capers, mayonnaise and lime juice together in a small bowl. Set aside.

5. Preheat the grill to medium. Toast the burger buns under the grill.

6. Heat the olive oil in a frying pan and cook the patties over a medium heat for 4–5 minutes on each side, until golden.

7. Spread the spicy mayonnaise over the bottom burger halves with a few sprigs of watercress and some slices of cucumber. Top with the burgers and sandwich with the second bun halves.

8. Serve with lime wedges for squeezing over the salmon burgers.

PER SERVING: 542 KCAL | FAT: 27.3 G | SAT FAT: 4.4 G | CARBS: 48.7 G | SUGARS: 4.1 G | FIBRE: 4 G | PROTEIN: 26.1 G | SALT: 1.2 G

TUNA & WASABI BURGERS

THESE TANTALIZING TUNA BURGERS ARE SERVED ON TOASTED CIABATTA, TOPPED WITH NUTRIENT-RICH PEPPERY WATERCRESS, WITH JAPANESE-INSPIRED PICKLED VEGETABLES ON THE SIDE.

 PREP TIME: 35 MINUTES, PLUS PICKLING | COOK TIME: 20 MINUTES | SERVES: 4

450 g/1 lb tuna steaks

25 g/1 oz fresh coriander, finely chopped

juice and zest of 1 lime

2 tsp wasabi paste

4 spring onions, finely chopped

4 tbsp mayonnaise

4 wholemeal ciabatta slices

1 tbsp olive oil, for brushing

100 g/3½ oz watercress

PICKLED VEGETABLES

4 tbsp rice wine vinegar

1 tbsp soft light brown sugar

125 ml/4 fl oz water

½ tsp coriander seeds, crushed

½ tsp mustard seeds

½ cucumber, sliced

2 carrots, cut into matchsticks

6 radishes, thinly sliced

3 shallots, thinly sliced

1. To make the pickled vegetables, place the vinegar and sugar with the water in a small saucepan over a high heat. Bring to a gentle simmer and stir until the sugar dissolves. Remove from the heat and add the coriander and mustard seeds. Place the cucumber, carrots, radish and shallots into a small bowl or sterilized jar. Pour over the pickling liquid and leave to cool and pickle for 4 hours or overnight.

2. Slice the tuna steaks into 2.5-cm/1-inch pieces and briefly pulse in a food processor until just chopped. Transfer to a large bowl and combine with the coriander, lime zest and juice, wasabi paste, spring onions and 2 tablespoons of the mayonnaise. Mix well and place in a refrigerator for 15 minutes.

3. Meanwhile, preheat a griddle pan over a medium—high heat. Griddle the ciabatta slices until toasted and set aside.

4. Shape the tuna mixture into four burger shapes and brush each with oil. Griddle for 6 minutes on each side, or until the burgers are cooked through.

5. Serve the tuna burgers on the toasted ciabatta slices, topped with the remaining mayonnaise and the watercress and with the pickled vegetables on the side.

PER SERVING: 356 KCAL | FAT: 10.2 G | SAT FAT: 1.5 G | CARBS: 34.4 G | SUGARS: 10.4 G | FIBRE: 4.9 G | PROTEIN: 32.4 G | SALT: 1.1 G

CLASSIC FISH BURGERS

YOU CAN VARY THE FISH YOU USE TO MAKE THESE BURGERS ACCORDING TO WHAT IS AVAILABLE – A MIXTURE OF FRESH AND SMOKED FISH WOULD PROVIDE A SOPHISTICATED TOUCH.

 PREP TIME: 15 MINUTES, PLUS CHILLING | COOK TIME: 25–30 MINUTES | SERVES: 4

450 g/1 lb floury potatoes, peeled and cut into chunks

450 g/1 lb mixed fish fillets, such as cod and salmon, skinned

2 tbsp chopped fresh tarragon

grated rind of 1 lemon

2 tbsp double cream

1 tbsp plain flour

1 egg, beaten

115 g/4 oz breadcrumbs, made from day-old white or wholemeal bread

4 tbsp vegetable oil, for shallow-frying

salt and pepper (optional)

15 g/¼ oz watercress, to serve

4 lemon wedges, to serve

1. Add the potatoes to a large saucepan of water, bring to the boil and cook for 15–20 minutes. Drain well and mash with a potato masher until smooth.

2. Meanwhile, put the fish in a frying pan and just cover with water. Place over a medium heat and bring to the boil, then reduce the heat, cover and simmer gently for 5 minutes, until cooked.

3. Remove from the heat and drain the fish onto a plate. When cool enough to handle, flake the fish into large chunks, ensuring that there are no bones.

4. Mix the potatoes with the fish, tarragon, lemon rind and cream. Season well with salt and pepper, if using, and shape into four large patties.

5. Dust the patties with flour and dip them into the beaten egg. Coat thoroughly in the breadcrumbs. Place on a baking tray and chill in the refrigerator for at least 30 minutes.

6. Heat the oil in the frying pan and fry the patties over a medium heat for 5 minutes on each side, turning them carefully with a palette knife or a fish slice.

7. Serve with the watercress, accompanied by the lemon wedges for squeezing over the fish burgers.

PER SERVING: 471 KCAL | FAT: 22.3 G | SAT FAT: 5 G | CARBS: 38.9 G | SUGARS: 3 G | FIBRE: 3.1 G | PROTEIN: 27.9 G | SALT: 0.6 G

SALMON BURGERS WITH PINE NUTS

FRESH SALMON, SPINACH AND PINE NUTS CREATE A VERY COLOURFUL AND DELICIOUS BURGER.

 PREP TIME: 15 MINUTES, PLUS CHILLING | COOK TIME: 25–35 MINUTES | SERVES: 4

300 g/10½ oz potatoes, cut into chunks

450 g/1 lb fresh salmon fillet, skinned

175 g/6 oz spinach leaves

55 g/2 oz pine nuts, toasted

2 tbsp finely grated lemon rind

1 tbsp chopped fresh parsley

2 tbsp wholemeal flour

200 ml/7 fl oz crème fraîche

4-cm/1½-inch piece cucumber, peeled and finely chopped

2 tbsp sunflower oil, for brushing

4 wholemeal buns, split

salt and pepper (optional)

28 cherry tomatoes, grilled to serve

1. Cook the potatoes in a saucepan of boiling water for 15–20 minutes, or until tender. Drain well, then mash and reserve. Chop the salmon into chunks.

2. Reserve a few spinach leaves for serving, then blanch the remainder in a saucepan of boiling water for 2 minutes. Drain, squeezing out any excess moisture, then chop.

3. Place the spinach in a food processor or blender with the salmon, potatoes, pine nuts, 1 tablespoon of the lemon rind, the parsley and salt and pepper to taste, if using. Blend together using the pulse button. Shape into four equal-sized burgers, then cover and leave to chill in the refrigerator for 1 hour. Coat the burgers in the flour.

4. Mix the crème fraîche, cucumber and the remaining lemon rind together in a bowl, then cover and leave to chill until required.

5. Preheat the barbecue to medium–high. Brush the burgers with the oil and cook for 4–6 minutes on each side, or until cooked through.

6. Place the reserved spinach leaves on the bottom halves of the buns and top with the burgers, then spoon over a little of the crème fraîche mixture. Add the lids and serve immediately with grilled cherry tomatoes.

PER SERVING: 798 KCAL | FAT: 49.9 G | SAT FAT: 16.2 G | CARBS: 53 G | SUGARS: 9.1 G | FIBRE: 8.5 G | PROTEIN: 37.1 G | SALT: 0.9 G

CHIPOTLE-LIME PRAWN BURGERS

THESE BURGERS ARE AN UNEXPECTED WAY TO EAT PRAWNS – AND A LIGHTER OPTION THAN MINCED BEEF.

PREP TIME: 15 MINUTES | COOK TIME: 10 MINUTES | SERVES: 4

550 g/1 lb 4 oz prawns, peeled and deveined

1 celery stick, finely diced

2 spring onions, finely chopped

2 tbsp chopped fresh coriander

1 garlic clove, finely chopped

½ tsp salt

½ tsp ground chipotle

juice and grated zest of 1 lime

2 tsp olive oil

2 tbsp reduced-fat mayonnaise

4 small wholemeal burger buns, split and toasted

4 Little Gem lettuce leaves

1. Process 450 g/1 lb of the prawns in a food processor. Dice the remaining 100 g/4 oz of prawns. In a medium bowl, combine the puréed and diced prawns. Add the celery, spring onions, coriander, garlic, salt, ground chipotle and lime zest and juice and mix well. Form the mixture into four burgers.

2. Heat the oil in a large, non-stick frying pan over a medium–high heat. Add the prawn burgers and cook for about 3–4 minutes or until browned underneath. Flip the burgers over and cook for a further 3–4 minutes or until browned and cooked through.

3. Spread the mayonnaise onto the lower halves of the buns, dividing evenly. Place one prawn burger on the lower half of each bun, then top with a lettuce leaf and the top half of the bun. Serve immediately.

PER SERVING: 254 KCAL | FAT: 7.9 G | SAT FAT: 1.4 G | CARBS: 25.3 G | SUGARS: 3.6 G | FIBRE: 3.8 G | PROTEIN: 20 G | SALT: 2.8 G

TUNA BURGERS WITH MANGO SALSA

FRESH TUNA, CHILLI AND MANGO ARE UNITED IN A TOTALLY MODERN BURGER.
TUNA IS BEST EATEN SLIGHTLY PINK AS IT CAN BE RATHER DRY IF OVERCOOKED.

 PREP TIME: 15 MINUTES, PLUS CHILLING | COOK TIME: 25–35 MINUTES | SERVES: 4

225 g/8 oz sweet potatoes, chopped

450 g/1 lb tuna steaks

6 spring onions, finely chopped

175 g/6 oz courgettes, grated

1 fresh red jalapeño chilli, deseeded and finely chopped

2 tbsp mango chutney

1 tbsp sunflower oil, for brushing

4 Little Gem lettuce leaves

MANGO SALSA

1 large ripe mango, peeled and stoned

2 ripe tomatoes, finely chopped

1 fresh red jalapeño chilli, deseeded and finely chopped

4-cm/1½-inch piece cucumber, finely diced

1 tbsp chopped fresh coriander

2 tsp clear honey

1. Cook the sweet potatoes in a saucepan of boiling water for 15–20 minutes, or until tender. Drain well, then mash and place in a food processor or blender. Cut the tuna into chunks and add to the potatoes.

2. Add the spring onions, courgette, chilli, and mango chutney to the food processor and, using the pulse button, blend together. Shape into four equal-sized patties, then cover and chill in the refrigerator for 1 hour.

3. Meanwhile make the salsa. Slice the mango, reserving 8–12 slices for serving. Finely chop the remainder, then mix with the tomatoes, chilli, cucumber, coriander and honey. Mix well, then spoon into a small bowl. Cover and leave for 30 minutes to allow the flavours to develop.

4. Preheat the barbecue to medium–high. Brush the burgers lightly with the oil and cook for 4–6 minutes on each side, or until piping hot. Serve immediately with the mango salsa, garnished with lettuce leaves and the reserved mango slices.

PER SERVING: 316 KCAL | FAT: 5.3 G | SAT FAT: 0.8 G | CARBS: 40.5 G | SUGARS: 25.6 G | FIBRE: 5.5 G | PROTEIN: 28.4 G | SALT: 2.5 G

POLENTA COD BURGERS WITH HOMEMADE AIOLI

PERKED UP WITH BASIL AND FRESH PARMESAN, THESE COD BURGERS ARE FANTASTICALLY TASTY. THE POLENTA THAT HOLDS ALL THE INGREDIENTS TOGETHER IS VERY EASY TO PREPARE.

 PREP TIME: 30 MINUTES, PLUS COOLING AND CHILLING | COOK TIME: 18–20 MINUTES | SERVES: 6

300 ml/10 fl oz water

225 g/8 oz instant polenta

450 g/1 lb cod fillets, skinned

1 tbsp chopped fresh basil

55 g/2 oz Parmesan cheese, grated

2 tbsp plain flour

2 tbsp olive oil, for brushing

6 wedges of ciabatta bread

baby spinach leaves and roasted Mediterranean vegetables (optional)

salt and pepper (optional)

AÏOLI

3 large garlic cloves, finely chopped

2 egg yolks

225 ml/8 fl oz extra virgin olive oil

1 tbsp lemon juice

1 tbsp lime juice

1 tbsp Dijon mustard

1 tbsp chopped fresh tarragon

salt and pepper (optional)

1. Place the water in a large saucepan and bring to the boil. Slowly pour in the polenta in a steady stream and cook over a gentle heat, stirring constantly, for 5 minutes or until thick. Leave to cool for about 10 minutes.

2. Place the polenta, fish, basil, cheese and salt and pepper, if using, in a food processor or blender and, using the pulse button, blend together. Shape into six equal-sized burgers, then coat in the flour. Cover and leave to chill in the refrigerator for 1 hour.

3. Meanwhile, make the aïoli. Ensure that all the ingredients are at room temperature. Place the garlic and egg yolks in a food processor and process until well blended. With the motor running, pour in the oil teaspoon by teaspoon through the feeder tube until the mixture starts to thicken, then pour in the remaining oil in a thin stream until a thick mayonnaise forms.

4. Add the lemon juice, lime juice, mustard and tarragon and season to taste with salt and pepper, if using. Blend until smooth, then transfer to a non-metallic bowl.

5. Cover with clingfilm and refrigerate until required.

6. Preheat the barbecue to medium–high. Brush the burgers with the oil and cook for 4–5 minutes on each side, or until cooked through.

7. Place each burger onto a ciabatta wedge and top with a spoonful of aïoli. Serve immediately with baby spinach leaves and roasted Mediterranean vegetables.

PER SERVING: 845 KCAL | FAT: 51.9 G | SAT FAT: 8.6 G | CARBS: 65 G | SUGARS: 2.4 G | FIBRE: 6.2 G | PROTEIN: 27.3 G | SALT: 1.1 G

TARTARE SAUCE FISH BURGER

THIS BURGER IS MADE WITH MAHI MAHI BUT OTHER WHITE FISH, SUCH AS POLLACK OR TILAPIA, WORK PERFECTLY WHEN MAHI MAHI ISN'T AVAILABLE.

 PREP TIME: 20 MINUTES, PLUS CHILLING | COOK TIME: 10 MINUTES | SERVES: 4

4 x 175 g/6 oz mahi mahi or other white fish fillets

2 tsp vegetable or rapeseed oil

4 soft burger buns, split

½ onion, sliced

4 Little Gem lettuce leaves

2 large tomatoes, sliced

salt and pepper (optional)

TARTARE SAUCE

2 small gherkin pickles, finely chopped

1 spring onion, finely chopped

1 tbsp capers, finely chopped

10 g/¼ oz fresh flat-leaf parsley, finely chopped

175 ml/6 fl oz mayonnaise

1 tbsp lemon juice

salt and pepper (optional)

1. To make the tartare sauce, put the pickles, spring onion, capers and parsley into a small bowl and stir in the mayonnaise.

2. Add the lemon juice and stir, then season with salt and pepper, if using. Cover and chill in the refrigerator for at least 30 minutes or up to 2 days before serving.

3. Rinse the fish and pat dry. Rub the fillets on both sides with the oil and sprinkle with salt and pepper, if using. Place on a large baking sheet.

4. Preheat the grill to high and place the rack about 8 cm/3¼ inches below the heat.

5. Place the fish on the rack and cook under the preheated grill for 4 minutes, then turn and cook for a further 3 minutes, or until the edges start to brown and the fish is just cooked through (the centre of the fish should flake easily when cut into).

6. Spread both halves of each bun with the tartare sauce. Place a fish fillet on each bun base and top with the onion slices, lettuce leaves and tomato slices. Add the bun lids and serve immediately.

PER SERVING: 635 KCAL | FAT: 36.9 G | SAT FAT: 5.8 G | CARBS: 32.5 G | SUGARS: 5.3 G | FIBRE: 4.1 G | PROTEIN: 38.5 G | SALT: 2 G

CRAB BURGERS

ONE BITE OF THESE CRAB BURGERS WILL TRANSPORT YOU TO THE SEASIDE,

 PREP TIME: 25 MINUTES, PLUS CHILLING | COOK TIME: 15 MINUTES | SERVES: 6

450 g/1 lb crabmeat

150 ml/5 fl oz mayonnaise

1 tbsp chopped fresh parsley

1 tsp Old Bay seasoning or other seafood seasoning mix

1 egg, beaten

1 tsp Worcestershire sauce

1 tsp mustard powder

½ tsp salt

¼ tsp pepper

30 g/1 oz dried breadcrumbs

2 tbsp butter

6 burger buns, split

4 Little Gem lettuce leaves, shredded

2 large tomatoes, sliced

tartare sauce and lemon wedges, to serve (optional)

1. Place the crabmeat into a medium-sized bowl and add the mayonnaise, parsley, Old Bay seasoning, egg, Worcestershire sauce, mustard, salt and pepper. Gently mix, then add the breadcrumbs, a little at a time, and mix very gently until combined. Chill in the refrigerator for at least 30 minutes.

2. Divide the mixture into six equal-sized portions and shape each portion into a patty.

3. Heat a ridged griddle pan over a medium heat, add the butter and heat until no longer foaming, stirring to coat the base of the pan. Add the patties and cook for about 6–7 minutes on each side until golden.

4. Put the burgers in the buns and top with the lettuce and tomato slices. Serve immediately with lemon wedges and tartare sauce, if using.

PER SERVING: 452 KCAL | FAT: 25.5 G | SAT FAT: 5.9 G | CARBS: 32.4 G | SUGARS: 4.6 G | FIBRE: 3.5 G | PROTEIN: 20.8 G | SALT: 3.3 G

PRAWN & CHIVE BURGERS WITH SWEETCORN RELISH

THIS RECIPE COULDN'T BE SIMPLER – OR TASTIER. GENTLY COOKING THE PRAWNS
OVER A MEDIUM HEAT HELPS KEEP THEM MOIST AND TENDER... AND UTTERLY DELICIOUS.

 PREP TIME: 40 MINUTES, PLUS CHILLING | COOK TIME: 30 MINUTES | SERVES: 4

450 g/1 lb raw prawns, peeled and deveined

25 g/1 oz chives, finely chopped

1 tsp vegetable oil

4 brioche buns, split

**SWEETCORN RELISH
(MAKES 950 G/2 LB 2 OZ)**

3 corn cobs

1 red pepper, deseeded and diced

1 jalapeño chilli, finely diced

125 ml/4 fl oz cider vinegar

100 g/3½ oz soft light brown sugar

1 tbsp salt

1 tbsp ground mustard seeds

½ tsp celery seeds

1 red onion, diced

1. Roughly chop the prawns, then place half in a food processor or blender and process until paste-like, or very finely chop with a knife. Stir the paste and chopped prawns together. Stir the chives into the prawns.

2. Divide the prawn mixture into four equal-sized portions. Using damp hands, shape each portion into a patty. Transfer the patties to a plate, cover and chill in the refrigerator for at least 30 minutes or overnight.

3. Meanwhile, make the sweetcorn relish. Cut the kernels off the corn cobs. Put the corn, red pepper, chilli, vinegar, sugar, salt, mustard seeds and celery seeds into a large saucepan over a medium–high heat and bring to the boil. Reduce the heat to simmering and cook, stirring occasionally, for about 15 minutes until the mixture reduces slightly. The sugar will melt, producing enough liquid to cover the vegetables.

4. Stir the onion into the corn mixture, remove from the heat and ladle the relish into sterilized jars. Seal with lids and leave to cool to room temperature. The relish will keep for up to 1 month in the refrigerator. Reserve 225 ml/8 fl oz the sweetcorn relish for the burgers.

5. Heat the oil in a large, non-stick frying pan over a medium heat and gently place the patties in the pan. Partially cover the pan and cook for 6 minutes until the patties are almost cooked through. Gently turn and cook on the other side for about 1 minute until pink and cooked through.

6. Place the burgers in the buns and top each with the reserved sweetcorn relish. Serve immediately.

PER SERVING: 391 KCAL | FAT: 12.9 G | SAT FAT: 5.9 G | CARBS: 49.1 G | SUGARS: 12.5 G | FIBRE: 2.8 G | PROTEIN: 18.3 G | SALT: 2.7 G

CHAPTER FIVE

SAUCES & SIDES

VEGAN TOMATO KETCHUP

TOMATO KETCHUP IS A HUGELY POPULAR STORECUPBOARD STAPLE AND MANY PEOPLE NEVER THINK TO MAKE THEIR OWN. THIS RECIPE IS SURPRISINGLY EASY AND TASTES SUPERB ATOP ANY OF THE BURGERS IN THIS BOOK.

 PREP TIME: 10 MINUTES | COOK TIME: 15–20 MINUTES | MAKES: ABOUT 250 ML/9 FL OZ

2 tbsp olive oil

1 red onion, chopped

2 garlic cloves, chopped

250 g/9 oz plum tomatoes, chopped

250 g/9 oz canned chopped tomatoes

½ tsp ground ginger

½ tsp chilli powder

40 g/1½ oz dark brown sugar

100 ml/3½ fl oz red wine vinegar

salt and pepper (optional)

1. Heat the olive oil in a large saucepan and add the onion, garlic and all the tomatoes. Add the ginger and chilli and season with salt and pepper, if using. Cook for 15 minutes, or until soft.

2. Pour the mixture into a food processor or blender and blend well. Sieve thoroughly to remove all the seeds. Return the mixture to the pan and add the sugar and vinegar. Return to the boil and cook until it is the consistency of ketchup.

3. Bottle quickly in sterilized bottles or jars and store in a cool place or refrigerator until required.

PER 250 ML/9 FL OZ: 575 KCAL | FAT: 28.9 G | SAT FAT: 3.7 G | CARBS: 72.2 G | SUGARS: 58.7 G | FIBRE: 6.3 G | PROTEIN: 7 G | SALT: 0.1 G

VEGAN SPICY SALSA

THIS SPICY, ROASTED SALSA MAKES A GREAT DIP FOR EVERYTHING FROM CHIPS TO ONION RINGS, AS WELL AS SPOONING OVER BURGERS.

 PREP TIME: 10 MINUTES | COOK TIME: 20 MINUTES | MAKES: ABOUT 450 ML/15 FL OZ

6 sprays of vegetable oil spray

8 plum tomatoes, halved

3 jalapeños, halved, cored and deseeded

4 garlic cloves

1 large onion, cut into wedges

25 g/1 oz fresh coriander

4 tbsp lime juice

salt (optional)

1. Preheat the oven to 230°C/450°F/Gas Mark 8 and spray a baking sheet with oil.

2. Place the tomatoes, jalapeños, garlic and onion on the prepared baking sheet and lightly spray with oil. Sprinkle with a little salt, if using, and roast in the preheated oven for about 15–20 minutes, until the vegetables soften and begin to brown.

3. Place the vegetables in a food processor and pulse to a chunky purée. Add the coriander, lime juice and 1 teaspoon of salt, if using, and pulse until the coriander is chopped and all of the ingredients are well combined.

4. To store, place in sterilized bottles or jars and refrigerate for up to 1 week.

PER 450 ML/15 FL OZ: 289 KCAL | FAT: 4 G | SAT FAT: 0.1 G | CARBS: 65.1 G | SUGARS: 29.9 G | FIBRE: 12.4 G | PROTEIN: 10.5 G | SALT: 0.1 G

MAYONNAISE

ONE OF THE BASIC SAUCES IN THE FRENCH REPERTOIRE, HOME-MADE MAYONNAISE
HAS A MILDER FLAVOUR THAN MOST SHOP-BOUGHT VARIETIES.

 PREP TIME: 5 MINUTES | COOK TIME: NO COOKING | MAKES: ABOUT 300 ML/10 FL OZ

2 large egg yolks

2 tsp Dijon mustard

2 tbsp lemon juice

300 ml/10 fl oz sunflower oil

salt and pepper (optional)

1. Whizz the egg yolks with the Dijon mustard, salt and pepper, if using, in a food processor or blender. Add the lemon juice and whizz again.

2. With the motor still running, add the oil, drop by drop at first. When the sauce begins to thicken, the oil can then be added in a slow, steady stream. Taste and adjust the seasoning with extra salt, pepper and lemon juice if necessary. If the sauce seems too thick, slowly add 1 tablespoon of hot water or lemon juice.

3. Use at once or store in a sterilized and airtight container in the refrigerator for up to 1 week.

PER 300 ML/10 FL OZ: 2774 KCAL | FAT: 309.4 G | SAT FAT: 34.1 G | CARBS: 3.8 G | SUGARS: 1 G | FIBRE: 0.4 G | PROTEIN: 5.8 G | SALT: 0.4 G

HOME-MADE MUSTARD

LIKE A SPICY COUNTRY-STYLE DIJON MUSTARD, THIS MUSTARD IS EASY TO MAKE BUT TAKES A FEW DAYS TO FINISH. THE FLAVOUR IMPROVES AND BECOMES LESS SPICY AFTER A COUPLE OF DAYS IN THE REFRIGERATOR.

 PREP TIME: 15 MINUTES, PLUS DEVELOPING | COOK TIME: NO COOKING | MAKES: 175 ML/6 FL OZ

3 tbsp brown mustard seeds

3 tbsp cider vinegar

1–2 tbsp water

3 tbsp mustard powder

2 tsp salt

2 tsp honey

1. Put the mustard seeds into a small, non-metallic container with the vinegar and enough water to cover completely. Set aside for two days, covered, at room temperature.

2. Strain the mustard seeds, reserving the liquid. Grind in a spice grinder until some seeds are still whole while some are ground. You may have to push the seeds down and grind again, but the more you grind, the spicier the mustard will be.

3. Place the mixture in a small bowl with the mustard powder, salt and honey. Add the reserved vinegar water and stir.

4. Place in a sterilized jar, seal and refrigerate for at least 2 days before serving.

PER 175 ML/6 FL OZ: 252 KCAL | FAT: 14.8 G | SAT FAT: 0.8 G | CARBS: 18.9 G | SUGARS: 14.2 G | FIBRE: 3.8 G | PROTEIN: 10.4 G | SALT: 12 G

VEGAN GUACAMOLE

A MEXICAN-STYLE DIP THAT IS DELICIOUS WITH A VARIETY OF THE BURGERS IN THIS BOOK OR ON THE SIDE FOR DIPPING CHIPS.

PREP TIME: 10 MINUTES | COOK TIME: NO COOKING | SERVES: 4

2 large avocados, stoned, peeled and sliced

juice of 2 unwaxed limes

2 large garlic cloves, crushed

1 tsp mild chilli powder, plus extra to garnish

salt and pepper (optional)

1. Put the avocado slices, lime juice, garlic and chilli in a food processor and process until smooth. Season with salt and pepper, if using.

2. Transfer to a serving bowl, garnish with chilli powder and serve immediately.

PER SERVING: 170 KCAL | FAT: 14.7 G | SAT FAT: 2.1 G | CARBS: 11.1 G | SUGARS: 1.1 G | FIBRE: 7.1 G | PROTEIN: 2.3 G | SALT: 0.8 G

VEGAN BEETROOT HUMMUS

THIS BRIGHTLY COLOURED HUMMUS IS PERFECT FOR SPREADING THICKLY ON TOP OF A VEGGIE OR CHICKEN BURGER.

PREP TIME: 15 MINUTES | COOK TIME: NO COOKING | SERVES: 6

400 g/14 oz canned chickpeas, drained and rinsed

1 garlic clove, roughly chopped

100 g/3½ oz cooked beetroot

1½ tbsp tahini

juice of ½ unwaxed lemon

3 tbsp olive oil

salt and pepper (optional)

1. Place the chickpeas, garlic and beetroot in a food processor or blender and process until broken into crumbs.

2. Add the tahini and lemon juice and process again, pouring in the oil until the hummus is the consistency you like. Season to taste with salt and pepper, if using, and serve.

PER SERVING: 212 KCAL | FAT: 14.3 G | SAT FAT: 1.9 G | CARBS: 15 G | SUGARS: 5.1 G | FIBRE: 4.8 G | PROTEIN: 5.3 G | SALT 0.1 G

VEGAN SPICY SRIRACHA SAUCE

THIS THAI-STYLE SUPER-SPICY SAUCE HAS A DELICIOUS FLAVOUR WITH JUST THE SAME CHILLI HIT AS SHOP-BOUGHT VARIETIES. PERFECT FOR ADDING AN EXTRA-SPICY KICK TO YOUR BURGER TOPPINGS.

 PREP TIME: 10 MINUTES, PLUS DEVELOPING | COOK TIME: 30 MINUTES | MAKES: ABOUT 175 ML/6 FL OZ

14 red jalapeño, serrano or Fresno chillies, stems removed and halved lengthways

1 red bird's eye chilli, deseeded

8 garlic cloves, coarsely chopped

3 tbsp soft light brown sugar

2 tbsp granulated sugar

2 tsp salt

6 tbsp white wine vinegar

1 tsp arrowroot

1. Put all the ingredients, except the vinegar and arrowroot, into a food processor or blender and finely chop. Transfer to a screw-topped jar large enough to hold the mixture with space at the top and seal. Leave to stand at warm room temperature, shaking once a day, for 2–4 days, or until the mixture becomes liquid.

2. Return the mixture to the food processor, add the vinegar and purée. Strain into a saucepan, rubbing backwards and forwards with a spoon and scraping the sieve to produce as much purée as possible.

3. Turn the extractor to high, or open a window to allow air to circulate. Place the pan over a medium heat, bring the purée to the boil and stir, until it is reduced by a quarter. Reduce the heat to low.

4. Dissolve the arrowroot with 1 tablespoon of the hot liquid, then stir it into the pan. Stir for 30 seconds, until the sauce thickens slightly. Set aside.

5. Leave to cool then leave to mature for 2 weeks in an airtight container in the refrigerator. The sauce will keep for 1 month in the refrigerator.

PER 175 ML/6 FL OZ: 624 KCAL | FAT: 3.2 G | TRACE SAT FAT | CARBS: 145.1 G | SUGARS: 108.9 G | FIBRE: 1.5 G | PROTEIN: 2.4 G | SALT: 12 G

CRISPY ONION RINGS

THE DELICIOUS, CRISPY COATING ON THESE ONION RINGS NICELY COMPLEMENTS THE SWEET TASTE OF THE ONION.

 PREP TIME: 5 MINUTES, PLUS STANDING | COOK TIME: 10 MINUTES | SERVES: 2

2 large white onions, peeled
150 g/5 oz plain flour
1 tsp paprika
1 egg
200 ml/7 fl oz fizzy water
15 g/¼ oz chopped fresh thyme
½ tsp salt
2 tbsp olive oil

1. Slice the onions into thick rings, and then pull apart the segments.

2. In a medium-sized bowl, whisk together the flour, paprika, egg and fizzy water. Add the thyme and season with salt. Leave for 5 minutes to thicken.

3. Heat the oil in a large non-stick frying pan over a medium heat. When the oil is hot, dip the onion rings in the batter, gently shake off the excess batter, then add to the pan. Cook the onion rings on both sides until golden and crispy. You may need to do this in 2 batches.

4. When the onion rings are cooked, drain on kitchen paper, and serve straight away.

PER SERVING: 393 KCAL | FAT: 15.8 G | SAT FAT: 2.4 G | CARBS: 53.9 G | SUGARS: 6.7 G | FIBRE: 4.8 G | PROTEIN: 9.2 G | SALT: 1.1 G

VEGAN CARAMELIZED ONIONS

SLICED ONIONS, COOKED SLOWLY UNTIL GOLDEN BROWN AND SLIGHTLY SWEET,
ARE A DELICIOUS ACCOMPANIMENT TO ALL KINDS OF BURGERS.

PREP TIME: 5 MINUTES | COOK TIME: 25 MINUTES | SERVES: 4

2 tbsp vegetable oil

½ red onion, sliced

½ tsp chopped fresh rosemary, thyme or oregano

½ tsp red wine vinegar

salt and pepper (optional)

1. Heat enough oil to coat the base of a large frying pan over a medium heat until shimmering. Add the onion and cook on one side for 3 minutes until brown. Add the herbs, stir and continue cooking, stirring occasionally, for about 12 minutes until nicely browned.

2. Season to taste with salt and pepper, if using. Add the vinegar and cook for a further 8–10 minutes until very soft.

3. Serve immediately or leave to cool and store in the refrigerator for up to 3 days.

PER SERVING: 66 KCAL | FAT: 6.8 G | SAT FAT: 0.7 G | CARBS: 1.4 G | SUGARS: 0.6 G | FIBRE: 0.2 G | PROTEIN: 0.2 G | TRACE SALT

VEGAN PICKLED ONIONS

THESE SWEET, SPICY AND TANGY ONIONS REQUIRE NO HEATING, SO THEY'RE EASY TO MAKE AT ANY TIME. INCLUDE THEM AT THE TABLE WITH ALL YOUR STANDARD BURGER CONDIMENTS.

 PREP TIME: 15 MINUTES, PLUS CHILLING | COOK TIME: NONE | MAKES: ABOUT 450 ML/16 FL OZ

225 ml/8 fl oz distilled white vinegar

100 g/3½ oz sugar

1 tsp chipotle powder, or to taste

2 red onions, cut into rings

salt (optional)

1. In a medium-sized bowl, combine the vinegar, sugar, chipotle powder, and salt to taste, if using. Whisk to dissolve the sugar.

2. Place the onions in a heavy-duty, zip-top polythene bag and pour the marinade over the onions. Toss to coat. Cover and refrigerate for 30 minutes, moving the mixture around a couple of times to evenly distribute the marinade. Drain before serving.

PER 450 ML/16 FL OZ: 531 KCAL | FAT: 0.8 G | SAT FAT: 0.1 G | CARBS: 123.8 G | SUGARS: 110.3 G | FIBRE: 4.9 G | PROTEIN: 3.2 G | SALT: 0.1 G

VEGAN CRANBERRY & RED CABBAGE COLESLAW

THIS VEGAN COLESLAW IS TOSSED WITH A TANGY ORANGE AND OLIVE OIL DRESSING. IT'S THE PERFECT HEALTHY ALTERNATIVE TO CHIPS TO SERVE ALONGSIDE ANY JUICY BURGER.

PREP TIME: 15 MINUTES | COOK TIME: 3 MINUTES | SERVES: 4

150 g/5½ oz red cabbage, thinly shredded

1 carrot, coarsely grated

140 g/5 oz cauliflower, cut into florets

1 red-skinned dessert apple, quartered, cored and very thinly sliced

40 g/1½ oz dried cranberries

50 g/1¾ oz alfalfa and sango radish shoots

DRESSING

50 g/1¾ oz walnuts, roughly chopped

juice of 1 unwaxed orange

4 tbsp virgin olive oil

2 tbsp chia seeds

salt and pepper (optional)

1. Put the red cabbage, carrot and cauliflower in a salad bowl. Add the apple, dried cranberries and shoots and toss well.

2. To make the dressing, put the walnuts in a large frying pan and toast for 2–3 minutes, or until just beginning to brown.

3. Put the orange juice, oil and chia seeds in a small bowl, season with salt and pepper, if using, then stir in the hot walnuts. Pour the dressing over the salad and toss. Serve immediately or cover and chill in the refrigerator until needed.

PER SERVING: 320 KCAL | FAT: 23.2 G | SAT FAT: 2.8 G | CARBS: 29.5 G | SUGARS: 16 G | FIBRE: 9.3 G | PROTEIN: 4.9 G | SALT: 0.8 G

VEGAN SPELT & CARROT SALAD

SERVE THIS HEALTHY SALAD IN A LARGE BOWL AT ANY BARBECUE FOR GUESTS TO ADD AS
AN EXTRA TOPPING TO THEIR BURGER OR FOR ADDED CRUNCH ON THE SIDE.

 PREP TIME: 15 MINUTES, PLUS STANDING | COOK TIME: 15 MINUTES | SERVES: 4

225 g/8 oz pearled spelt, rinsed

½ tsp salt

2 tbsp fresh thyme leaves

40 g/1½ oz toasted pine nuts

5 spring onions, thinly sliced

4 carrots

3 tbsp salad cress, to serve

DRESSING

2 tbsp orange juice

1 tbsp lemon juice

2-cm/¾-inch piece fresh ginger, squeezed in a garlic press, juice reserved

2 tsp soy sauce

6 tbsp extra virgin olive oil

salt and pepper (optional)

1. Put the spelt and salt into a saucepan with plenty of water to cover. Bring to the boil, then reduce the heat, cover and simmer for 10 minutes, until tender but still chewy. Drain, then spread out on a tray to cool slightly. Tip into a serving bowl while still lukewarm.

2. To make the dressing, combine the orange juice, lemon juice and ginger juice in a small bowl. Add the soy sauce. Season to taste with salt and pepper, if using. Whisk in the oil.

3. Pour the dressing over the spelt, mixing gently with a fork. Stir in the thyme, pine nuts and spring onions.

4. Using a vegetable peeler, shave the carrots into thin ribbons, discarding the woody core. Add to the spelt mixture.

5. Leave to stand at room temperature for 30 minutes to allow the flavours to develop. Sprinkle with the cress just before serving.

PER SERVING: 464 KCAL | FAT: 28.2 G | SAT FAT: 3.5 G | CARBS: 48.7 G | SUGARS: 5.4 G | FIBRE: 6.2 G | PROTEIN: 9.5 G | SALT: 1.2 G

ZESTY AVOCADO & ALMOND SALAD

SMOOTH AND TASTY AVOCADOS ARE FLAVOURED WITH ZESTY LEMON JUICE, FRAGRANT CORIANDER, PIQUANT SPRING ONIONS AND HOT CHILLI, AND GIVEN AN ADDED CRUNCH WITH A SPRINKLING OF FLAKED ALMONDS.

PREP TIME: 10–15 MINUTES | COOK TIME: 5 MINUTES | SERVES: 4

2 tsp olive oil

55 g/2 oz flaked almonds

1 iceberg lettuce, quartered and torn into bite-sized pieces

3 avocados, halved, stoned and peeled

juice of 2 lemons

DRESSING

4 tbsp low-fat natural yogurt

2 spring onions, finely chopped

¼ tsp dried crushed red chillies

25 g/1 oz fresh coriander, finely chopped

salt and pepper (optional)

1. Heat the oil in a frying pan over a medium heat. Add the almonds and cook for 3–4 minutes, or until golden, stirring often, then leave to cool.

2. Put the lettuce in a salad bowl. Slice two of the avocados, put them in a bowl and squeeze over the juice of 1½ lemons to prevent discolouration. Transfer them to the salad bowl.

3. To make the dressing, mash the remaining avocado on a plate with the remaining lemon juice. Mix in the yogurt, spring onions, dried chillies and coriander and season lightly with salt and pepper, if using.

4. Sprinkle the salad with the cooked almonds, then spoon the dressing over the salad. Serve immediately alongside your burgers.

PER SERVING: 289 KCAL | FAT: 24 G | SAT FAT: 3.2 G | CARBS: 17.8 G | SUGARS: 5.4 G | FIBRE: 9.7 G | PROTEIN: 6.9 G | SALT: 0.1 G

POTATO SALAD

COOL AND CREAMY, THIS SALAD SHOULD BE AN INTEGRAL PART OF ANY BARBECUE.

 PREP TIME: 20 MINUTES, PLUS CHILLING | COOK TIME: 30 MINUTES | SERVES: 8

1.25 kg/2 lb 12 oz waxy potatoes

125 ml/4 fl oz mayonnaise

50 ml/2 fl oz soured cream

90 ml/3 fl oz white wine vinegar

1 tsp wholegrain mustard

½ tsp dried dill

75 g/2¾ oz red onions, finely chopped

30 g/1 oz celery, finely chopped

30 g/1 oz gherkins, chopped

40 g/1½ oz roasted red peppers, chopped

2 medium hard-boiled eggs, chopped (optional)

salt and pepper (optional)

1. Place the unpeeled potatoes in a medium-sized saucepan and cover with water by a few inches. Add salt, if using, bring to the boil over a high heat, then reduce the heat and simmer for 20–30 minutes until fork-tender.

2. Put the mayonnaise, soured cream, vinegar, mustard, dill, and salt and pepper, if using, into a bowl and mix together.

3. Drain the potatoes and leave to cool slightly, then slip off the skins with your fingers or with a paring knife. Chop the potatoes into 1-cm/½-inch pieces and add to the dressing while still warm. Stir in the onion, celery, gherkins, peppers and eggs, if using. Cover and chill for at least 2 hours or overnight.

PER SERVING: 246 KCAL | FAT: 13.1 G | SAT FAT: 2.5 G | CARBS: 29.2 G | SUGARS: 2.3 G | FIBRE: 3.6 G | PROTEIN: 3.7 G | SALT: 0.4 G

MACARONI CHEESE

THIS SATISFYING FAVOURITE GOES WELL WITH ANY BURGER. SPOON ON TOP OF YOUR PATTY OF CHOICE FOR ADDED FLAVOUR AND CREAMY TEXTURE.

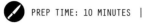 PREP TIME: 10 MINUTES | COOK TIME: 35 MINUTES | SERVES: 4

250 g/9 oz dried macaroni pasta

½ tbsp butter

600 ml/1 pint full-fat milk

½ tsp grated nutmeg

55 g/2 oz butter

55 g/2 oz plain flour

200 g/7 oz Cheddar cheese, grated

55 g/2 oz Parmesan cheese, grated

salt and pepper (optional)

1. Bring a large saucepan of water to the boil. Add the pasta, bring back to the boil and cook for 8–10 minutes, or until tender but still firm to the bite. Remove from the heat and drain. Add ½ tbsp butter, return to the pan and cover to keep warm.

2. Put the milk and nutmeg into a separate saucepan over a low heat and heat until warm, but do not bring to the boil.

3. Melt the remaining butter in a heavy-based saucepan over a low heat, then add the flour and stir to make a roux. Cook gently for 2 minutes.

4. Add the milk a little at a time, whisking it into the roux, then cook for a further 10–15 minutes to make a loose, custard-style sauce.

5. Add three quarters of the Cheddar cheese and all the Parmesan cheese and stir through until they have melted in. Season to taste with salt and pepper, if using, then remove from the heat.

6. Preheat the grill to high. Put the macaroni into a shallow heatproof dish, then pour the sauce over.

7. Scatter the remaining cheese over the top and place the dish under the preheated grill. Grill until the cheese begins to brown. Serve immediately.

PER SERVING: 743 KCAL | FAT: 38.8 G | SAT FAT: 23.5 G | CARBS: 66.5 G | SUGARS: 9.6 G | FIBRE: 2.4 G | PROTEIN: 30.8 G | SALT: 1.7 G

BURGER BUNS

THE BUNS ARE JUST AS IMPORTANT AS THE BURGERS INSIDE THEM. YOU'LL DEFINITELY NOTICE THE DIFFERENCE FROM SHOP-BOUGHT BUNS WHEN YOU BITE INTO THESE DELIGHTS.

 PREP TIME: 20 MINUTES, PLUS RESTING | COOK TIME: 15–20 MINUTES | MAKES: 8 BUNS

450 g/1 lb strong white bread flour

1½ tsp salt

2 tsp caster sugar

1 tsp easy-blend dried yeast

150 ml/5 fl oz lukewarm water

150 ml/5 fl oz lukewarm milk

10 g/¼ oz strong white bread flour, for dusting

15 ml/1 tbsp vegetable oil, for brushing

3 tbsp sesame seeds

1. Sift the flour and salt together into a bowl and stir in the sugar and yeast. Make a well in the centre and pour in the lukewarm water and milk. Stir well with a wooden spoon until the dough begins to come together, then knead with your hands until it leaves the side of the bowl. Turn out on to a lightly floured surface and knead well for about 10 minutes, until smooth and elastic.

2. Brush a bowl with oil. Shape the dough into a ball, put it in the bowl and put the bowl into a plastic bag or cover with a damp tea towel. Leave to rise in a warm place for 1 hour, until the dough has doubled in volume.

3. Brush two baking sheets with oil. Turn out the dough on to a lightly floured surface and knock back with your fist. Divide it into eight equal-sized pieces, shape each into a ball and put them on the prepared baking sheets. Flatten slightly with a lightly floured hand and put the baking sheets into plastic bags or cover with damp tea towels. Leave to rise in a warm place for 30 minutes.

4. Preheat the oven to 200°C/400°F/Gas Mark 6. Lightly press the centre of each bun with your fingers to release any large air bubbles. Brush the tops with the oil and sprinkle with sesame seeds. Bake for 15–20 minutes, until light golden brown. Transfer to wire racks to cool.

PER SERVING: 260 KCAL | FAT: 4.8 G | SAT FAT: 0.9 G | CARBS: 43.1 G | SUGARS: 2.5 G | FIBRE: 1.9 G | PROTEIN: 10.2 G | SALT: 1.1 G

BUTTERMILK BURGER BUNS

THESE SLIGHTLY SWEET AND SOFT-TEXTURED BUNS WILL SANDWICH ANY BURGER PERFECTLY.

 PREP TIME: 30 MINUTES, PLUS RESTING | COOK TIME: 10–20 MINUTES | MAKES: 8 PIECES

400 g/14 oz strong white flour

150 g/5½ oz plain flour

100 g/3½ oz butter, diced

1 large egg

2 tbsp sugar

7 g/¼ oz dried yeast

300 ml/10 fl oz buttermilk

1 tsp salt

10 g/¼ oz plain flour, for dusting

1 egg, lightly beaten, for glazing

1. In a large bowl, mix the strong white flour and plain flour together and rub in the butter until the mixture resembles fine breadcrumbs.

2. In a medium-sized bowl, whisk together the egg, sugar, yeast, buttermilk and salt.

3. Pour the egg mixture into the flour mixture and combine using the back of a wooden spoon. Turn out the dough onto a floured surface and knead for 10 minutes, or until elastic and smooth.

4. Place the dough in a clean bowl, cover with clingfilm and leave in a warm place to rise for 1½ hours.

5. Knock back the dough, then turn out onto a floured surface. Divide the mixture into 8 pieces. Roll each piece into a ball and place on a large baking tray, spaced well apart to allow the buns to double in size.

6. Cover the tray with clingfilm and leave in a warm place for 30–40 minutes, or until doubled in size. Preheat the oven to 180°C/350°F/Gas Mark 4.

7. Lightly brush the buns with the beaten egg and bake in the preheated oven for 15–20 minutes.

PER SERVING: 403 KCAL | FAT: 13.7 G | SAT FAT: 7.7 G | CARBS: 56 G | SUGARS: 5.9 G | FIBRE: 2 G | PROTEIN: 13.1 G | SALT: 1.1 G

VEGAN HAND-CUT CHIPS

CRISPY HAND-CUT CHIPS ARE THE PERFECT ACCOMPANIMENT TO ANY BURGER. COOKING THEM IN THE OVEN IS MUCH HEALTHIER THAN FRYING.

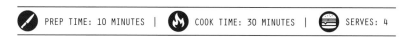 PREP TIME: 10 MINUTES | COOK TIME: 30 MINUTES | SERVES: 4

900 g/2 lb potatoes, cut into even sticks

2 tbsp vegetable oil

1 tsp sea salt

1. Preheat the oven to 230°C/450°F/Gas Mark 8.

2. Toss the cut potatoes with vegetable oil and sea salt.

3. Spread the chips in a single layer on a large baking sheet and bake in the preheated oven for about 30 minutes, flipping them halfway through cooking, until they are golden brown and crisp.

4. Serve immediately alongside your burger of choice.

PER SERVING: 233 KCAL | FAT: 7 G | SAT FAT: 0.7 G | CARBS: 39.3 G | SUGARS: 1.8 G | FIBRE: 4.7 G | PROTEIN: 4.6 G | SALT: 1.5 G

VEGAN GARLIC CHIPS

CLASSIC HAND-CUT CHIPS HIT WITH A PUNGENT DOSE OF FRESH GARLIC AND A SPRINKLING OF CHOPPED PARSLEY.

PREP TIME: 15 MINUTES | COOK TIME: 30 MINUTES | SERVES: 4

900 g/2 lb potatoes
2 tbsp vegetable oil
1 tsp sea salt
1 tbsp olive oil
3 large garlic cloves, finely chopped
2 tbsp finely chopped fresh flat-leaf parsley
sea salt (optional)

1. Preheat the oven to 230°C/450°F/Gas Mark 8. Peel the potatoes, if desired, and cut into even sticks.

2. Toss the potato sticks with vegetable oil and sea salt.

3. Spread the chips in a single layer on a large baking sheet and bake in the preheated oven for about 30 minutes, flipping them halfway through cooking, until they are golden brown and crisp.

4. Whisk together the oil, garlic and parsley in a large bowl.

5. Toss the hot chips with the garlic mixture. Season generously with sea salt, if using, and serve immediately alongside your burger of choice.

PER SERVING: 267 KCAL | FAT: 10.4 G | SAT FAT: 1.2 G | CARBS: 40.2 G | SUGARS: 1.9 G | FIBRE: 4.8 G | PROTEIN: 4.8 G | SALT: 1.5 G

SMOKY PAPRIKA
SWEET POTATO CHIPS

STARCHY AND SWEET, WITH CRUNCHY EDGES AND FLUFFY INSIDES, THESE CHIPS MAKE A REALLY SATISFYING
ACCOMPANIMENT TO ANY BURGER. ALWAYS USE THE BEST PAPRIKA YOU CAN FIND.

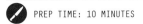 PREP TIME: 10 MINUTES | COOK TIME: 40 MINUTES | SERVES: 2

300 g/10½ oz sweet potatoes,
unpeeled, scrubbed and cut
into chips

2 tbsp olive oil

1 heaped tbsp smoked paprika

sea salt and pepper (optional)

SOURED CREAM DIP

4 stalks of chives, finely snipped

150 g/5½ oz soured cream

salt and pepper (optional)

1. Preheat the oven to 180°C/350°F/Gas Mark 4. Put the sweet potatoes, oil and smoked paprika in a large bowl, season with salt and pepper, if using, and toss well.

2. Arrange the chips in a single layer on a large baking sheet. Bake for 30–40 minutes, or until crisp.

3. To make the dip, put the chives and soured cream in a bowl and mix. Season with salt and pepper, if using, and divide between two small dipping bowls.

4. Line two larger bowls with kitchen paper. Transfer the chips to the bowls and serve immediately with the dip alongside your burger of choice.

PER SERVING: 399 KCAL | FAT: 28.4 G | SAT FAT: 10.4 G | CARBS: 32.8 G | SUGARS: 8.8 G | FIBRE: 5 G | PROTEIN: 4 G | SALT: 1.1 G

THAI RED CHIPS

THESE UNUSUAL OVEN-BAKED FRIES HIT ALL THE RIGHT TASTE BUDS — SWEET, SPICY, TANGY, SALTY, AND ALL-AROUND DELICIOUS.

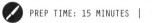 PREP TIME: 15 MINUTES | COOK TIME: 30 MINUTES | SERVES: 4

2 tbsp vegetable oil,
plus 15 ml/1 tbsp for greasing

2 tbsp soft light brown sugar

2 tbsp Thai fish sauce

2 tbsp lime juice

1 tbsp Thai red curry paste

½ tsp cayenne pepper (optional)

900 g/2 lb potatoes, cut into
even sticks

CORIANDER KETCHUP

1 garlic clove

15 g/½ oz fresh coriander

225 ml/8 fl oz tomato ketchup

2 tbsp lime juice

1. Preheat the oven to 230°C/450°F/Gas Mark 8. Grease a large baking sheet with oil.

2. Put the oil, sugar, fish sauce, lime juice, curry paste and cayenne pepper, if using, into a mixing bowl and stir together until well combined.

3. Add the potato sticks to the mixture in the bowl and toss to coat. Leave to stand for about 5 minutes, then, using a slotted spoon, transfer the potatoes to the prepared baking sheet, allowing the excess marinade to run off into the bowl. Spread the potatoes in a single layer. Bake in the preheated oven for 25–30 minutes, turning after about 15 minutes, until brown and crisp.

4. Meanwhile, to make the ketchup, chop the garlic and coriander in a food processor. Add the ketchup and lime juice and process until well combined. Transfer to a serving bowl.

5. Serve the chips hot with the ketchup for dipping, alongside your burger of choice.

PER SERVING: 366 KCAL | FAT: 10.9 G | SAT FAT: 1.1 G | CARBS: 65.5 G | SUGARS: 22.3 G | FIBRE: 5.4 G | PROTEIN: 5.9 G | SALT: 3.4 G

VEGAN STUFFED POTATO SKINS

SERVE THESE VEGAN POTATO SKINS ALONGSIDE YOUR BURGERS FOR A FILLING DINNER OPTION.

 PREP TIME: 10–15 MINUTES | COOK TIME: 35 MINUTES | SERVES: 2

1 tbsp vegetable oil, for greasing

2 baking potatoes

2 tbsp olive oil, for brushing/frying

3 vegan bacon-style rashers

1 tbsp chopped fresh mixed herbs, such as sage, parsley, oregano

10 g/¼ oz vegan margarine

salt and pepper (optional)

1. Preheat the oven to 190°C/375°F/Gas Mark 5. Lightly grease a baking sheet with vegetable oil.

2. Score a ring around each potato, in the place where you will eventually cut them in half. Wrap them in kitchen paper and microwave for 6–10 minutes, or until cooked through. Unwrap and leave until cool enough to handle. Cut the potatoes in half and carefully scoop out the flesh, leaving a shell around 1 cm/½ inch thick. Set the flesh aside in a medium bowl.

3. Brush the outside of the potato skins with 1 tbsp olive oil and place them, cut-side down, on the prepared baking sheet. Bake in the preheated oven for 15 minutes, or until browned, then remove from the oven and transfer to a clean baking sheet, cut-side up.

4. Heat the remaining olive oil in a frying pan over a medium heat. Fry the rashers for 5 minutes, or until crisp, and then chop finely or crumble them. Mash the reserved potato flesh with a fork, and then mix in the rashers and chopped herbs. Season to taste with salt and pepper, if using.

5. Preheat the grill to high. Pile the mashed potato back into the potato skins, make ridges on top with a fork and dot with a little vegan margarine. Place under the hot grill for 5 minutes until the tops are golden and crisp. Serve immediately.

PER SERVING: 460 KCAL | FAT: 25.5 G | SAT FAT: 4.4 G | CARBS: 46 G | SUGARS: 2.1 G | FIBRE: 6.8 G | PROTEIN: 13.1 G | SALT: 0.5 G

BACON & CHEESE LOADED CHIPS

THESE LOADED CHIPS ARE PUMPED FULL OF FLAVOUR WITH ONION, GARLIC, TWO KINDS OF CHEESE, CRUMBLED BACON, AND FRESH CHIVES.

 PREP TIME: 15 MINUTES | COOK TIME: 45 MINUTES | SERVES: 4

3 streaky bacon rashers

3 tbsp butter

½ onion, diced

1 garlic clove, finely chopped

3 tbsp plain flour

350 ml/12 fl oz milk

280 g/10 oz mature Cheddar cheese, grated

55 g/2 oz Parmesan cheese, grated

125 ml/4 fl oz soured cream

2 tsp Dijon mustard

salt (optional)

2 tbsp snipped fresh chives, to garnish

HAND-CUT CHIPS

900 g/2 lb potatoes, cut into even sticks

2 tbsp vegetable oil

1 tsp sea salt

1. Preheat the oven to 230°C/450°F/Gas Mark 8. Fry the bacon in a dry frying pan until crisp, then remove and drain on kitchen paper. Crumble and set aside.

2. Melt the butter in a saucepan over a medium heat. Add the onion and cook, stirring, for about 4 minutes, until soft. Add the garlic and cook for a further minute. Whisk in the flour and cook for a further 30 seconds. Slowly add the milk and cook over a medium heat, whisking constantly, for a further 3 minutes, until the sauce thickens. Reduce the heat to low and add the Cheddar cheese and Parmesan cheese 25 g/1 oz at a time, stirring after each addition, until the cheese is completely melted. Stir in the soured cream, mustard and salt, if using. Keep the sauce warm until ready to serve.

3. To make the hand-cut chips, toss the potato sticks with vegetable oil and sea salt.

4. Spread the chips in a single layer on a large baking sheet and bake in the preheated oven for about 30 minutes, flipping them halfway through cooking, until they are golden brown and crisp.

5. Place the chips in a large bowl or on a serving platter and pour over the sauce. Sprinkle with the crumbled bacon and chives and serve immediately.

PER SERVING: 820 KCAL | FAT: 53.7 G | SAT FAT: 27.4 G | CARBS: 53.8 G | SUGARS: 8.3 G | FIBRE: 5.2 G | PROTEIN: 32.2 G | SALT: 3.8 G

VEGAN BUTTERNUT SQUASH WITH SAGE & PUMPKIN SEEDS

A HEALTHY AND COLOURFUL ALTERNATIVE TO A SIDE PORTION OF CHIPS.

 PREP TIME: 20 MINUTES | COOK TIME: 35 MINUTES | SERVES: 3

1 large butternut squash

1 tbsp olive oil

½ tsp chilli powder

12 fresh sage leaves, finely chopped

50 g/1¾ oz pumpkin seeds

salt and pepper (optional)

1. Preheat the oven to 200°C/400°F/Gas Mark 6. Prepare the butternut squash by washing any excess dirt from the skin and slicing off the very top and very bottom.

2. Using a sharp knife and a steady hand, cut the squash into six long wedges. Scoop out any seeds and discard. Place the wedges on a baking tray. Brush with half of the olive oil and sprinkle with the chilli powder. Roast in the preheated oven for 25 minutes.

3. Remove from the oven and brush with the remaining olive oil. Sprinkle over the sage and pumpkin seeds. Season with salt and pepper, if using, and return the wedges to the oven for a further 10 minutes. Serve immediately, garnished with extra pepper, if using.

PER SERVING: 259 KCAL | FAT: 13.3 G | SAT FAT: 2.1 G | CARBS: 33.9 G | SUGARS: 6.1 G | FIBRE: 7.2 G | PROTEIN: 7.8 G | TRACE SALT

CHICKPEA TOFU STICKS
WITH SPICY DIP

COTTAGE CHEESE IS A FRESH CURD THAT'S DRAINED BUT NOT PRESSED, SO SOME OF THE WHEY REMAINS. AS THE BASE OF A SPICY DIP, IT TASTES AMAZING DUNKED OVER STRIPS OF HOMEMADE TOFU.

 PREP TIME: 15 MINUTES, PLUS STANDING AND CHILLING | COOK TIME: 5–6 MINUTES | SERVES: 4

90 g/3¼ oz gram flour

1 tsp miso paste

½ tsp ground turmeric

500 ml/18 fl oz water

SPICY DIP

300 g/10½ oz cottage cheese

1 tbsp mayonnaise

2 tsp creamed horseradish

½ tsp Dijon mustard

1 spring onion, trimmed and finely chopped

12 olives, stoned and finely chopped

1. To make the chickpea tofu, place the gram flour in a bowl with the miso paste and turmeric. Whisk in 250 ml/9 fl oz of the water.

2. Bring the remaining water to the boil in a saucepan. When the water is boiling, pour the gram flour mix into the pan and start whisking.

3. Simmer while stirring constantly, until the mixture thickens. Pour it into a 15-cm/6-inch square tin or dish. Leave to stand at room temperature for 20 minutes, then chill in the fridge for at least 30 minutes.

4. Meanwhile, make the dip by combining the ingredients in a small bowl.

5. Cut the tofu into strips and serve with the spicy dip.

PER SERVING: 208 KCAL | FAT: 8.9 G | SAT FAT: 1.9 G | CARBS: 18.7 G | SUGARS: 5.9 G | FIBRE: 3.2 G | PROTEIN: 13.3 G | SALT: 1.1 G

VEGAN ROASTED KALE CRISPS

KALE'S MEATY FLAVOUR BECOMES WONDERFULLY INTENSE WHEN THE LEAVES ARE ROASTED. TORN INTO BITE-SIZED PIECES, THEY MAKE CRISPY MORSELS THAT ARE PERFECT SERVED WITH JUICY BURGERS.

PREP TIME: 15 MINUTES | COOK TIME: 15 MINUTES | SERVES: 4

250 g/9 oz kale

2 tbsp olive oil

2 pinches of sugar

2 pinches of sea salt

2 tbsp toasted flaked almonds,
to garnish

1. Preheat the oven to 150°C/300°F/Gas Mark 2. Remove the thick stems and central rib from the kale (leaving about 125 g/4½ oz trimmed leaves). Rinse and dry very thoroughly with kitchen paper. Tear into bite-sized pieces and place in a bowl with the oil and sugar, then toss well.

2. Spread about half the leaves in a single layer in a large roasting tin, spaced well apart. Sprinkle with a pinch of sea salt and roast on the bottom rack of the preheated oven for 4 minutes.

3. Stir the leaves, then turn the tray so the back is at the front. Roast for a further 1–2 minutes, until the leaves are crisp and very slightly browned at the edges. Repeat with the remaining leaves and sea salt. Sprinkle the kale crisps with the flaked almonds and serve immediately.

PER SERVING: 119 KCAL | FAT: 9.7 G | SAT FAT: 1.1 G | CARBS: 6.8 G | SUGARS: 2.1 G | FIBRE: 2.7 G | PROTEIN: 3.6 G | SALT: 0.8 G

INDEX